THE PRACTICE OF CHRISTIAN HEALING

A Guide for Beginners

Roy Lawrence

InterVarsity Press
Downers Grove, Illinois

$1.00

InterVarsity Press® is the book-publishing division of InterVarsity Christian Fellowship®, a student movement active on campus at hundreds of universities, colleges and schools of nursing in the United States of America, and a member movement of the International Fellowship of Evangelical Students. For information about local and regional activities, write Public Relations Dept., InterVarsity Christian Fellowship, 6400 Schroeder Rd., P.O. Box 7895, Madison, WI 53707-7895.

All Scripture quotations, unless otherwise indicated, are taken from the HOLY BIBLE, NEW INTERNATIONAL VERSION®. NIV®. Copyright © 1973, 1978, 1984 by International Bible Society. Used by permission of Zondervan Publishing House. All rights reserved.

Cover photograph: Gary Braasch
ISBN 0-8308-1960-6

Printed in the United States of America ∞

Library of Congress Cataloging-in-Publication Data

Lawrence, Roy, 1931-
   The practice of Christian healing: a guide for beginners/by Roy
Lawrence.
      p.   cm.
   Includes bibliographical references (p.   ).
   ISBN 0-8308-1960-6 (pbk.: alk. paper)
   1. Spiritual healing.   I. Title.
BT732.5.L335   1996
234'.13—dc20
                                                              96-19409
                                                                      CIP

| 18 | 17 | 16 | 15 | 14 | 13 | 12 | 11 | 10 | 9 | 8 | 7 | 6 | 5 | 4 | 3 | 2 | 1 |
| 11 | 10 | 09 | 08 | 07 | 06 | 05 | 04 | 03 | 02 | 01 | 00 | 99 | 98 | 97 | 96 |

To Judy, Jim, Caroline
and Christopher Noakes
in whose home so many have found
Christian healing

—*ONE*—

HERE AM I, LORD—SEND SOMEBODY ELSE!

*I*n my stock of religious jokes there is one which is just a question and answer:

Question: How do you make God laugh?

Answer: Tell him your future plans!

If there is any truth in this joke, I must have given the Almighty many a laugh in my time.

As a nonchurchgoing teenager I unexpectedly found myself deciding to become a serious Christian. I clearly remember kneeling down by the side of my bed and saying a prayer like this: "Lord, I want to put my life in your hands and to do whatever you want me to do, but there's just one thing I want to say to you. Please don't ever ask me to be a parson. I couldn't stand that. But apart from that, you name it, Lord, and I'll try to do it."

Over forty years later, here I am sitting at the desk in my vicarage, writing with one hand and fingering my dog-collar with the other. That's the trouble with God. You just can't trust him—not when you are offering him service with strings attached.

In my twenties, when I had finally accepted my call to the ministry, I tried it again with him. I told him that if I was to go into the ministry, I could not see myself as a long-serving parish clergyman. I thought I would be best as a quick-in-and-out man, zooming into a parish, sorting it out and then zooming out again, leaving the work of consolidation to someone else.

Presumably there was another heavenly guffaw, and as I sit at my desk the thought comes to me that very soon I shall become the longest-serving vicar in the whole history of my Merseyside parish of Prenton, Birkenhead!

Another thing that I was sure about, as I studied for my degree in classics and theology at Oxford and then went on to obtain a Cambridge Ordination Certificate, was that I never wanted to have anything to do with the overemotional, oversensational, overgullible side of religion—and I put spiritual healing firmly into that category. The young woman I was to marry, who was a trained medic, a chartered physiotherapist, was of exactly the same opinion. We both regarded spiritual healing as a dubious concept smacking of hocus-pocus and superstition.

How are the mighty (or the not-so-mighty) fallen! As I sit at my desk to start work on my eighth book, five of them have been about some aspect or other of the ministry of Christian healing, and my wife, Eira, is now just as committed to this ministry as I am.

None of this came easily to us. I was precipitated into thinking about the healing ministry, against all my expectations, when one day I was in a car full of clergy on the way to a conference in Blackpool. Quite suddenly and casually someone said, "Have you noticed that when Jesus says 'preach,' he usually adds 'and heal'?"

Preach and Heal

It was just a chance comment, but for me it proved a seminal thought. I could not get rid of it. It went into my mind and started to disturb me, because if Jesus has given his followers two equally important commands, "preach" and "heal," then a church which hears only half his commission is lopsided and incomplete.

I was due to go back to Oxford for a refresher course, so I decided to spend part of the time researching the healing ministry. I found that healing is a primary biblical topic, that it was an integral element in the life of the early church and that most of the clergy who were in the refresher course with me could tell stories of spiritual healing— though, like myself, they had relegated them to the periphery of their ministry.

The more I studied the evidence, the surer I became that healing cannot be regarded properly as a peripheral subject. I knew that when I returned to my parish I must introduce it into the heart of our worship pattern. Since my faith that any healing service of mine would actually have results was minimal, the Sunday evening monthly service which I introduced into the parish bore the hesitant title "Investigation into Christian Healing."

It all sounds pretty detached and cautious to me now, but at the time it was too much for my wife, Eira. She was afraid I might be plunging into the sort of irrational religious emotionalism which she most disliked and feared. She also thought it sounded distinctly risky and unsound from a medical standpoint. She went so far as to say that my involvement in spiritual healing could well endanger our marriage, and when I offered her a laying on of hands for the slipped disc which had troubled her for some years, she told me in no uncertain terms just what I could do with my hands!

In fact ultimately her back was completely healed at a healing service, but initially you could not have imagined two less likely enthusiasts for the Christian healing ministry. Our motto was "Here am I—send somebody else!"

Actually, it is beginning to dawn on me that God knew what he was doing in all of this. I do believe that God is calling the whole church to rediscover the ministry of Christian healing, but it has to be a sensible, balanced, scriptural ministry. It must not in any way be unreal, because it has to reflect the One who reveals the essence of reality, the One who is "the way, the truth and the life." So the natural caution and skepticism which both Eira and I felt had a legitimate role in the discovery of the ministry which was to change our lives.

Five Tests

It is my conviction that the Christian healing ministry (like every other form of ministry) should pass five tests of truth if it is to be acceptable.

1. It must be true to the Scriptures taken as a whole.

2. It must be true to all that we know of Jesus.

3. It must be true to reason—because God gave us minds and presumably means us to use them.

4. It must be true to experience, and this must include personal experience, the experience of history and the traditional experience of the church.

5. It must be true to the promptings of the Holy Spirit in us.

I invite you to apply these five tests to every statement this book contains.

I hope I have been equipped to apply the first test not only by my years of academic theology, but also by the love of Scripture which has never ceased to grow in me.

I hope never to stray from the parameters of the second test, because my definition of Christian healing is that its basic nature is simply *the difference made by Jesus when he meets us at our point of need.*

As one who is a rationalist by temperament, I would hope that the third test would always have a place in my assessment procedure. Intellectual integrity means a great deal to me, though I have to admit that the study of Christian healing does take me from time to time into realms with which my powers of reason are not equipped to deal.

I hope that my years of steady parish ministry have given me sufficient experience to know which things actually work out in practice and that the fourth test will never allow me the dangerous luxury of wishful thinking or dogmatic blindness.

As for the fifth test, I can only pray "Come, Holy Spirit" on writer and reader alike.

The purpose of the pages that follow will be to look at the nature, the purpose, the potential of Christian healing, and to ask how it works—if it does. Of course, if there is no truth and power in this ministry, this must be discerned. Clearing the clutter of falsehood and fantasy from religious belief and practice is certainly something Jesus would approve of. It would be dreadful to allow a gigantic confidence trick to become part of the established ministry of the Christian church.

However, if, as I now believe, there are truth and power in the Christian healing ministry, then to fail to discern the truth and channel the power would be a betrayal. It would be a betrayal of this world in which sickness of body, mind and spirit is so dangerously evident and which needs all the healing it can get. It would be a betrayal of the church, which has been commissioned by its Founder to preach and heal. Above all, it would be a betrayal of Jesus himself, who would not have given us this commission unless along with it he knew he could enable us to continue his mission on earth.

— T W O —

WHAT IS
CHRISTIAN HEALING . . .
& WHAT IS IT NOT?

When I was a teenager, a phrase in the *Times Literary Supplement* made a big impression on me. I remember the exact words. "Theology," it said, could be "an attractive, exciting and fascinating quest."

At the time I was still very much a beginner in the Christian faith. Many of my friends thought theology was boring, and it was not long since I had thought so too. It was, of course, a nonsensical opinion, because theology is the study of God, and if God exists, the one thing he cannot be is boring. Whatever you and I find most interesting and captivating and wonderful in the whole world can be no more than a pale reflection of the God who made everything. He has to be mind-bendingly, soul-ravishingly marvelous. To seek him and find him has to be the greatest adventure in the world. Any theology which is not "an attractive, exciting and fascinating quest" is no theology at all. It is not a study of God but a betrayal of God.

However, before becoming too euphoric at the thought of launching another investigation into God in the pages of this book, I would do well to add a fourth adjective to the quotation from the *Times Literary Supplement.* Theology is not only attractive, exciting and fascinating. It is also *dangerous.* Terrible things have been done in the name of religion. Terrible ideas have been propagated in the name of religion.

Avoiding the Minefields
There are minefields of wrong ideas to be negotiated in exploring any area of Christian thought or practice. An investigation into Christian healing is no exception. So, before asking what Christian healing is and how and whether it works, it makes sense to clear the way by making sure we know what Christian healing is *not.*

1. First, let it be absolutely and abundantly clear that Christian healing is not a venture into magic or a flirtation with the occult. Its results can seem amazing and sometimes even miraculous, but it works within God's self-consistent laws. The more committed I become to the Christian healing ministry, the more suspicious I become of those things which have the flavor of the occult.

2. I am also convinced that Christian healing is not a ministry which is confined to those who have special "gifts," though special gifts do exist—both *natural* gifts (innate abilities and talents) and *spiritual* gifts (charisms).

There seems no reason to dispute that some people have a natural gift of healing. Mysteriously, something flows from them which does other people good. I am told that it can actually be recorded on film by Kirlian photography. But God is frequently pleased to use people who have absolutely no awareness of a gift of this sort.

Any Christian who is conscious of such a gift can and should offer it to God, just as any other gift can be offered to God—a gift of music or art or mathematical aptitude. Our gifts come from God and are enhanced when we offer them back to him.

Personally, I have been aware of having a gift of music from a very early age and have sought to offer it to God and use it in his service. But to the best of my knowledge I have no natural gift of healing, and I am rather grateful for that fact. If I had a natural gift of healing, I might start to put my trust in *it* rather than in the Lord himself, and I am glad not to have that temptation.

Natural gifts of healing offered to God in the name of Jesus can have a place in the total ministry of Christian healing, but I believe it is a small place.

The same is true even of "charismatic" gifts. Some people find that when they become Christians they become aware of new abilities and talents, which they regard as specific gifts from the Holy Spirit. One of my former colleagues found, after she became a Christian, that quite unexpectedly she was given the capability to paint lovely pictures; she has used this ability ever since in God's service.

Some of these gifts are related to the ministry of healing. For instance, in a nearby parish there is a vicar who seems to have a diagnostic gift. If he passes his hands over the body of someone who comes to him for help, keeping his hands an inch away from their skin, he finds that when he comes to an area where there is a problem, somehow he knows it. He can even know it before the sufferer becomes consciously aware of it. I knew another clergyman who did something similar at a mental level. He had a gift of what he called "hunches"—hunches that could be uncannily accurate. When someone came to him for counseling, he could sometimes know the root of the trouble as soon as the person walked through his study door. It could be unnerving for him— and even more so for those he counseled!

Some healing evangelists display a similar aptitude in a packed room. They can sense needs and predict healings among the people present. I remember being at such a meeting where the evangelist pointed (apparently) straight at me and named a medical condition which was in need of healing. Fortunately, from my point of view, the man behind me immediately stood up and admitted the condition. I hope he went on to receive healing.

Many believe that St. Paul refers to phenomena such as these when he writes about "gifts of healings" in 1 Corinthians 12:9. They have their part in the ministry of healing, but, once again, my conviction is that it is not a major part. Christian healing is not a peripheral ministry confined to a few people with personal gifts, whether they are natural or charismatic. In this book I shall be arguing that Christian healing is not basically a ministry for "stars" or specialists, but that it is a ministry for the whole body of Christ, and that God calls every Christian congregation and every Christian individual to have a role in it, with or without a personal gift of healing.

3. The ministry of Christian healing is not dependent on "supersaintliness" on the part of the ministrants; you don't have to be holier than other Christians to take part in it.

As I write these words, I am beginning the twentieth year of my time as vicar of the parish of Prenton. By now I know my congregation well and they know me well. We know each other's faults, failings and foibles. We know that we are very ordinary Christians. If extraordinary holiness were a prerequisite of involvement in the healing ministry, we would not be used in the way that we are.

Christian healing can be an extraordinary ministry, but ordinary Christians are called to it. Even brand-new Christians who are just beginning their own life of discipleship can be used as channels of the healing power of Jesus. Jennifer Rees Larcombe was suddenly and spectacularly healed after eight years of chronic disablement and constant pain with encephalitis. Christian healing came to her through the nervous and reluctant word and touch of a new Christian. Jennifer Rees Larcombe tells the story in her moving book *Unexpected Healing.*

4. It is also important to know that Christian healing is more than just one among many forms of "alternative medicine." Alternative therapies are fashionable these days, and some people seem to think that there is little difference between one and another. However, these forms of treatment are a very mixed bag.

They remind me of a poem I used to recite when I was a toddler:

There was a little girl
Who had a little curl
Right in the middle of her forehead.
When she was good
She was very very good
But when she was bad, she was horrid.

When alternative therapies are good, they can be very good indeed, but when they are bad they can be decidedly sinister. It depends on what comes with the package.

Some are based mainly on an affirmation of the fundamental value of every human being and of God's creation as a whole. They rely on lots and lots of TLC (tender loving care), which cannot be other than good. Others use techniques which at this stage are regarded as medically unorthodox, but which have a practical value and which after research may well one day be accepted as normal medical procedure. This happened, for instance, over the years to the techniques of physiotherapy.

However, there are other alternative therapies in which recipients may get more than they bargain for, because the treatment conceals a hidden agenda. Sufferers may, for instance, go to a so-called "spiritual healer" and find themselves unexpectedly enmeshed in the world of spiritism with its mediums and spirit guides. They may go to yoga classes, thinking of them simply as a good way to learn to practice relaxation, and then find themselves absorbing Buddhist philosophies and beliefs. They may even find an underlay of witchcraft or Satanism beneath an alternative therapy. I would guess that Satan would regard it as a good bargain if he were to heal a person's body but could corrupt that person's soul in the process.

Against this varied background, Christian healing is absolutely unique, as can be seen by turning to the end of this chapter. Fuzzy thinking that confuses it with other therapies should be resisted.

5. It is also important to see the difference between Christian healing and faith healing. Many people confuse the two. They stop me in the street and ask, "How are the faith healing services going, Vicar?" They are surprised when I tell them that what we do in church is not faith healing.

Faith healing is a form of auto-suggestion. Auto-suggestion, if I understand it rightly, is based on the belief that the human mind is very powerful and can influence the material and physical, and that if you believe something strongly enough, you can make it so. If you say a few prayers around this process, you can turn the auto-suggestion into faith healing. The healing agent in faith healing is faith itself.

There is limited truth in this, but Christian healing is much more. In Christian healing, though the ministrant must have faith, it is neither the ministrant's faith nor the recipient's faith which does the healing. In Christian healing, faith is no more than a channel. Healing power flows through it but comes from another source. We shall see in chapter five that the source is no less than God the Father, God the Son and God the Holy Spirit.

6. If the power base of the Christian healing ministry is the Holy Trinity, then this ministry cannot be unorthodox, weird or newfangled. The message of Christian healing is not an alternative to the traditional gospel of the Christian church. It is part and parcel of that gospel. If it were not so, personally I would want to have nothing to do with it.

Christian healing services should reflect the whole breadth of the Christian tradition and not be confined to any single type. They can be high-church, low-church or middle-church. They can be traditional or modern. They can be charismatic or noncharismatic, liturgical or informal. They can and should reflect the ethos of the church in which they are taking place. They should lead to a rediscovery of the healing power of *all* worship and demonstrate that *all* services should be healing in some way.

7. It is perhaps also worth saying that just as Christian healing is not an unorthodox concept theologically, so it is not unorthodox medically. It is not meant to discourage anyone from seeking medical care, and there is nothing in it at all which is incompatible with good medical practice. We will look at this in greater detail in chapter four.

So then, if Christian healing has no connection with magic or with the occult, if it is not a ministry dependent on special gifts, if it is not dependent on superholiness, if it is more than just one among many forms of alternative medicine, if it is more than faith healing, and if it is not at variance with either theological or medical orthodoxy—if it is none of these things, what actually is it?

I believe the answer is breathtakingly simple.

Christian healing is the difference that Jesus Christ makes in body, mind, spirit and lifestyle for those who take him seriously.

Bishop Morris Maddocks, adviser in the ministry of Christian healing to the Archbishops of Canterbury and York, was once asked during the course of an interview to define Christian healing. Rather to his own surprise he found himself saying these words in reply: "Christian healing is Jesus Christ meeting you at the point of your need."

There could not be a better answer.

It has always been a fundamental Christian conviction that the dynamic behind the life of a believer lies in his or her encounter and union with Jesus. To pray as a Christian is to practice Christ's presence. To worship together with other Christians is to discover Jesus in the midst. To live as a Christian is to walk and talk with Jesus day by day. This is no mere figure of speech. It is the heart of the Christian faith that Christ is risen and that he has given his followers a very precise promise: "I am with you always, to the very end of the age" (Mt 28:20).

The Christian healing ministry is based on an acceptance of this promise and a working out of its implications.

Healing, First-Century Style

During the earthly ministry of Jesus, when he met people he was never a nonevent. Those who met him in the first century A.D. were different afterward. He was "infectious" with wholeness. In the words of Matthew, Jesus went about "preaching the good news of the kingdom, and healing every disease and sickness among the people" (4:23). He made a difference to people physically, but the difference was much deeper than that. Not only did the lame walk, the deaf hear and the blind see, but new peace and sanity came to those who were mentally and emotionally tormented, and tarnished evildoers became clean and new. Lifestyles were transformed. Aims and attitudes were changed. There was a new relationship with people and with God. St. Paul wrote, "If anyone is in Christ, he is a new creation" (2 Cor 5:17).

That was Christian healing, first-century style. It is still the essence of the Christian healing ministry. If Christ is risen, and if you and I can meet him, and if he has not changed but is the same yesterday, today and forever (Heb 13:8), then logically we should expect that an encounter with him can and will make the same sort of difference that it always did.

In a nutshell, Christian healing is practicing the presence of Jesus and expecting him to be "the same"—no more and no less.

—THREE—

DOES CHRISTIAN HEALING REALLY WORK?

*T*he scriptural basis for the Christian healing ministry seems to me to be irresistible. I am amazed and rather ashamed that I managed to ignore it for so many years.

We have seen that it rests first on the command which Jesus gave to his followers to preach *and heal*. Those who wish to read a minihandbook on the authority for the ministry of Christian healing can do no better than to read chapters 8, 9 and 10 of Luke's Gospel.

In chapter 8 we read that Jesus undertook a personal mission of preaching and healing. There is great teaching, including the parable of the sower. Three remarkable healings are recorded. A disturbed and violent man in a graveyard was restored to peace and sanity. A woman with years of chronic hemorrhage was healed. A young girl, presumed dead, was restored to life by the presence, word and touch of Jesus.

The disciples must have been amazed at this ministry and must have thought it totally unique—until to their astonishment they heard him authorize and command them to share it. They too were to heal people! "He sent them out to preach the kingdom of God and to heal the sick" (Lk 9:2). To their surprise they found themselves "preaching the gospel and healing people everywhere" (v. 6).

Now it was the turn of other Christians to be amazed at the fact that the Twelve could share Christ's work and power. But in chapter 10 Jesus commanded *all* the followers who happened to be with him to be involved in it. He sent out seventy-two people with the twofold command ringing in their ears: "Heal the sick who are there and tell them, 'The kingdom of God is near you' " (v. 9).

This commission was rapidly extended to all believers. Jesus commanded "those who believe" to "place their hands on sick people" and promised that healing would take place (Mk 16:17-18).

James pictures the healing ministry of an ordinary Christian congregation in these words: "Is any one of you sick? He should call the elders of the church to pray over him and anoint him with oil in the name of the Lord. And the prayer offered in faith will make the sick person well; the Lord will raise him up. If he has sinned, he will be forgiven. Therefore confess your sins to each other and pray for each other so that you may be healed" (Jas 5:14-16).

Jesus' Guarantee

For a Christian the clear scriptural commands should be sufficient to launch us into a ministry of healing, but Jesus, in his graciousness, has not left this as a matter of mere obedience. To his command he has added a solemn promise. "Where two or three come together in my name, there am I with them" (Mt 18:20). "I am with you always, to the very end of the age" (Mt 28:20). So in the Christian healing ministry there is need for only one Healer, and that is Jesus himself, whose presence is personally guaranteed. In the words of explorer David Livingstone, "This is the word of a gentleman of the most sacred and strictest honour, and there's an end on't."

The command and promise of Jesus on which the Christian healing ministry is founded are not found in an isolated corner of Scripture. I now see the Bible as *primarily* concerned with healing, not just physical healing but healing which can touch humankind at every level—body, mind, spirit, attitudes, relationships, personal life, corporate life, healing in time and healing for eternity. I hope one day to produce a book which will be an overview of the whole Bible from this standpoint. The title which comes to mind is *A Change of Leaves,* because the Bible begins with the "leaves of shame" with which Adam and Eve cover their nakedness when they have lost their oneness with God, with each other and with their own inner integrity, but it ends with the "leaves of healing" on the tree of life in the final chapter of the book of Revelation.

In between the beginning of Genesis and the end of Revelation, Scripture tells the story of the way in which this change of leaves comes about. In the Old Testament God selects a people to learn about his healing and saving purposes and offers them six channels through which this insight can come to them: the channel of experience, the channel of law, the temple with its pattern of worship, the wisdom literature with its philosophy of life, the prophets, and a promise of One who is to come who will uniquely embody God's work and will. Then the New Testament tells of the fulfillment of the healing potential of these channels in Christ, the church and the kingdom. And it invites us to take our part in this healing and saving process here and now.

But What If It Doesn't Work?

If all of this is true, if Christian healing is based on the command and promise of Jesus himself, if it covers the whole of life and is one with the whole of Scripture, why is there hesitation about the ministry on the part of some Christians—or to put it personally, why did I resist for years what now seems to me to be the heart of the Christian gospel and the plain message of Scripture?

I think the answer is very simple. I was not sure that it would actually work in practice. I found myself asking, "Supposing it all goes wrong? Will it damage the faith of my congregation? Will it damage my own faith? How can I be sure what will happen?"

To be honest, you can't be sure that the ministry of Christian healing will always work *as we desire.*

As Paul Tournier has written in *A Doctor's Casebook,* "God is not at *our* service. To claim to penetrate His secrets, know His signs and have His power at our beck and call is not faith, but magic" (London: SCM Press, 1954, p. 87).

However, though Christian healing is never a venture into magic, that does not mean it is a puny or powerless ministry.

The rest of this chapter contains stories of healing, and there will be still more in the remainder of the book. I include them with some degree of hesitation, because on the whole Jesus avoided publicity, and because the sort of healing ministry which gives the impression of sensationalism, glory-seeking and infallibility has always made me cringe. However, it may be helpful and encouraging for any who are hesitating on the brink of the healing ministry to know the sorts of things that can happen in an ordinary church and an ordinary ministry like my own when the command of Jesus to preach *and heal* is taken seriously.

I believe that if any congregation perseveres in the Christian healing ministry, sooner or later various sorts of healing can be expected.

Healing of the Body

Some healings will be physical. When Jesus sent a message to John the Baptist to help him deal with the doubts and depression he was feeling in prison, much of that message contained reminders of physical healings. "Go back and report to John what you hear and see: The blind receive sight, the lame walk, those who have leprosy are cured, the deaf hear" (Mt 11:4-5).

Elsewhere I have written about the first three categories in this list and the way in which instances of these healings can still be found within the life and ministry of the church today, but so far I have not written about the restoration of hearing by Christian healing. Let me now try to remedy that omission.

A couple of years ago my wife and I were invited to conduct schools of healing prayer in the Isle of Man, an island in the Irish Sea halfway between Britain and Ireland. It was a remarkable occasion on which we saw healings which felt as though they could have come straight out of the New Testament. At one stage, we had forty or fifty people engaged in a meditation on the healing work of the Holy Spirit. This prayer method is described in my book *How to Pray When Life Hurts* (Downers Grove, Ill.: InterVarsity Press, 1993, p. 77). My wife noticed one of the women present, Lydia, gazing out of a window with an expression of sheer delight.

Afterward, during the "report back" session, Lydia told us the reason. For some time her hearing had been deteriorating. Initially she criticized her husband for mumbling, but when she could no longer hear the birds sing, she realized that *they* could not be mumbling; she was going deaf. As the people around her at the school of prayer received and transmitted the Holy Spirit, she found herself praying, "Lord, if you have some Holy Spirit power to spare, please, I do need some for myself. Can you do something for my deafness?" As she prayed she felt movements within her inner ear, and quite suddenly her hearing was restored. The immediate proof was that she could now hear the birds singing outside the church window. She was thrilled to tell us about it, and we were all able to praise God together.

It brought back to mind an occurrence in my early days in Prenton.

We had just started healing services, and one of our choirboys was not sure he believed a word I said on these occasions. However, Nigel's granny was almost stone deaf. She was driving the family to distraction by insisting that the TV should be turned up to maximum volume. The family could hardly speak or think for the noise. So Nigel found himself coming forward to a laying on of hands and praying, "Lord, this is for Granny. I don't know whether there is anything in this Christian healing, but if there is, can you do anything about Granny's deafness, because it's driving us mad." When he arrived home an hour later the volume of the TV had been turned down to normal, and his mother said, "Nigel, you'll hardly believe it, but while you were in church Granny's hearing came back."

Some months ago I was conducting a midweek Communion service and the Gospel for the day happened to be the famous "Ephphatha" story in which Jesus restored hearing to a deaf man (Mk 7:31-37). Always in the past when I had preached on this story, I had turned it into a parable and taught that God wants to open the deaf ears of the world to his Word and to open the blocked lips of the church so that we become better messengers of the gospel. All of this is true, of course, but the primary meaning of the story is much more literal. It teaches that Christian healing can include healing the deaf, and on this occasion I felt moved to say so.

When I returned to the vicarage, there were two visitors for coffee. One was Joy, wife of the vicar of a neighboring parish. The other was Sally, a friend who was staying with her. Sally was just about to offer herself as a uniformed member of the Salvation Army, but she had a problem. She was stone deaf in one ear, and her situation was made worse by continuous severe tinnitus (a sensation of ringing noises in the inner ear). She was not sure that with this disability she could be of service in the way she felt called. Her doctor had told her that he knew of no cure for her condition.

With the words of my sermon still ringing in my own ears, I felt I had to ask her if she had ever sought the ministry of Christian healing. Sally answered with a firm "No!" (rather to my relief, I am ashamed to admit), and the two of them went on their way. However, she obviously thought about the question, because before she ended her stay she asked Joy and her husband and their two daughters to lay hands on her in the name of Jesus.

The day after she returned home, she phoned Joy with the news that her tinnitus had disappeared and that she was holding the telephone receiver to her stone-deaf ear and hearing perfectly. Her doctor was amazed and said that medically speaking it seemed that the impossible had happened.

These are fairly representative stories of the way in which Christian healing can have a physical impact. Sometimes, however, its effect is on the mind rather than the body.

Healing of the Mind

Two years ago I was invited to give a talk about Christian healing at our local branch of the manic-depressive society. After the talk one of the women present, Lill, came with her husband and asked to talk to me. Lill said that though for many years she had been diagnosed as manic depressive, she had always had a conviction that one day she would meet somebody who would bring her healing. She now believed I was that person. We talked together for some time, and then I gave her a laying on of hands with prayer in the name of Jesus. A year later she telephoned to tell me that the hospital which she had long attended had told her that for some reason which they could not understand she could no longer be regarded as manic depressive and that she would not need to be seen there again.

A further illustration of the healing of the mind by the power of Christ can be found in some detail in chapter five of *How to Pray When Life*

Hurts, which tells the story of Meryl, who had been written off as incurably mentally ill by the doctors she had seen, though she was herself a doctor, but who was restored by the ministry of Christian healing and is now working again and finding that her own patients are now benefiting from the spiritual truths she herself has learned.

Healing at a Spiritual Level

Sometimes the healing is not so much physical or mental as spiritual and affects attitudes, relationships, faith and faithlessness, convictions and lifestyle.

Shortly after I became vicar of Prenton, the British Broadcasting Corporation invited me to present two television programs from our parish church explaining and exemplifying the ministry of Christian healing. The first was an exposition of the facts and included testimonies from four people who had received healing through this ministry. There was a dentist who, when in the hospital with a life-threatening condition of double-virus pneumonia, found that his soaring temperature immediately reverted to normal after I visited his ward and laid hands on him in the name of our Lord. There was a woman whose severe arthritis went into spectacular remission for ten years after a healing service. There was a man with a knee condition which prevented him from dancing, playing badminton and kneeling to say his prayers, who found he could do all these after a Christian healing service. The knee condition has not returned. Finally there was a woman who had been disabled for eleven years by a steadily deteriorating condition of multiple sclerosis, which is usually thought to be incurable. Her condition improved markedly after receiving the ministry of Christian healing. After two years of steady improvement she was told by her hospital that she could no longer be said to have MS. They were all interviewed by David Davies, a well-known BBC personality.

The second program was an actual Christian healing service. As the laying on of hands took place in church, viewers were invited to practice the presence of the healing Christ in the privacy of their own homes and in this way to involve themselves in the Christian healing experience.

Admittedly these two programs focused primarily on physical healing. There was an extraordinary response. To my surprise and to the surprise of the BBC, six hundred people either wrote or phoned to tell me of the impact that the programs had had on them. Many reported that they had been touched in some way by the message and power of these services.

But healing of the spirit happened as well. Out of all these reactions, the two letters which moved me most were both from men who were atheists. In each case they told me that as they watched the programs they felt faith return to them. This too was Christian healing in action.

I suppose that if I were to put my mind to it I could fill the rest of this book with similar stories of healings of body, mind or spirit by the power of Christ.

Although we have no magic wand, Christian healing is a remarkable ministry because Jesus is a remarkable Savior. It is an available ministry because he is an available Savior. It makes a difference because he makes a difference. It can be life-transforming because he is life-transforming. In my own limited experience I know that Christian healing can and does work, and I would betray that experience as well as the truth of Scripture if I were to say otherwise.

I know that my call is to seek to understand Christian healing but never to manipulate it. I must seek to channel it but never to exploit it.

And this, I believe, is God's call to us all.

—FOUR—

COMMENTS
FROM A MEDICAL
STANDPOINT

*I*t is common for conferences on the church's healing ministry to
begin with a session that looks for basic definitions and asks the question "What *is* Christian healing?"

I find that there are two ways in which this session can be handled.
One is by a piece of exposition like that in chapter two of this book.
The other (which can be effective if there are not too many in the
group) is by discovering an answer from the personal life stories of
members of the conference. All those who have allowed Jesus into their
lives in any real sense are invited to share with the group any difference
which they are aware he has made in them. Usually most are able to
speak in some specific way of answers to prayer, changes in lifestyle,
challenges to prejudice, healings of relationships, new courage, new
peace, new purpose, new awareness, differences in body, mind and
spirit. In this way we are able to define Christian healing out of the

experience of the group itself.

One conference at which Eira and I were speaking got off to a startling beginning when one man said, "I can certainly speak about the power of Jesus and the difference he can make, because he healed my wife of cancer. It was supposed to be terminal, but, at the first healing service ever held at our local church, she received a laying on of hands in the name of Christ from our own vicar and a local doctor. Afterward x-rays showed that the cancer had disappeared."

The woman next to him said, "I can confirm that because I am his wife!"

A Doctor Who Believed

Then the man next to her said, "And I can confirm it because I am the doctor who laid hands on her. Afterward I made it my business to look at her medical records, and there is no doubt either about the cancer or about its disappearance."

It is rare to find instant medical confirmation of Christian healing in this way. More often stories of Christian healing are characterized by doctors as "anecdotal." Some would regard many of the stories in this book in this way, in spite of the care I have tried to take in telling them. In view of this, it would not be surprising to find a high degree of caution on the part of doctors in assessing the phenomenon of Christian healing. However, in my own experience I find that there is an increasingly positive response to this ministry in medical circles.

An example is the service of Christian healing we held in our parish just two weeks ago. It was attended by about 120 people, and a dozen of them were medical workers of one sort or another. They included four doctors, a physiotherapist and several nurses. And they were all totally at home in our worship and totally at ease with the teaching.

Once a year Eira and I attend a residential conference arranged by the Acorn Christian Healing Trust for the purpose of dialogue about the healing ministry. Well over a hundred people are usually present, and normally about 50 percent come from a medical background. On these occasions I have never known there to be discord between those who are medically trained and those who have a theological background.

From time to time I am invited to speak at medical gatherings about the spiritual dimension in healing. Always those present receive me with courtesy and keen attention.

Two years ago a rather daunting medical group in Nottingham invited me to visit them and to speak on "The Interface of Medicine and the Church" or "When the Church and the Medics Meet." To prepare myself I went to visit Peter Ashton, a doctor who has recently retired from a Welsh country practice. He is both a friend and an enthusiast for the Christian healing ministry.

He and I went for a walk in the fields and woods around Montgomery, where he lives, and he gave me his advice about the talk I was going to give to his colleagues. I owe much of the remainder of this chapter to him.

The Spiritual Dimension

He suggested that a good starting point for any consideration of healing is the question "What is man?" Physicians have many treatments for the body. Psychiatrists have many treatments for the mind. But can they care for the whole needs of human beings? That depends on whether a person is more than just body and mind—whether there is a deep center of being that is greater than physical and mental chemistry, a "spiritual core." It cannot be proved, but many people (doctors included) find it necessary to accept it as a working hypothesis.

By chance there was a letter in the *London Times,* just a few days before I gave my talk, from a doctor urging the necessity of accepting the "spiritual." He wrote, "The religious instinct of the ages accepts a dimension of spirit that goes beyond physics and chemistry. Life is more than digesting food, viewing TV and wrestling with computer data."

If this is true, that to understand humankind we have to think in physical, mental and spiritual terms, then to understand wholeness we have also to think physically, mentally and spiritually. And if we are to find healing for our hurts, we will need those who can help us at all three levels of our being.

We know that the three aspects of our being interrelate. The body affects the mind and the spirit, as in the case of a postnatal depression or the effects a dose of flu can have on our attitudes and emotions. Similarly the mind and spirit affect the body: skin rashes can be brought about by guilt or anxiety, or a cherished resentment can spoil our appetite, stop us from sleeping, clog our bodies with catarrh or constipation, and exacerbate any tendencies we may have to asthma or arthritis. Because of this interrelationship, it makes sense that those who are skilled in the physical, mental and spiritual disciplines should work together.

Church and Medicine Working Together

What has the church to offer within this healing partnership?

First, we can offer the gift of time. Doctors in Britain are often conscious of the limitations they face due to a lack of time—and so are their patients. My doctor friend from Montgomery told me how for many years he had struggled to allocate an average of ten minutes to each patient who came to his office. He found it inadequate, but it was better than the widespread British practice of keeping the average appointment to five minutes only! By contrast, though I am a busy vicar I can usually allocate a full hour to people who come to me with a problem, and certainly never less than half an hour. In addition, I have the resource of a congregation behind me, and some of them have time and perhaps professional skills at their disposal. They can be invaluable in areas such as postbereavement care.

Second, we can give the gift of ordinary concern and care. Any society which is deprived of these qualities will be sick at heart. If the churches can increase the level of practical loving, this is bound to have a healing impact on the community as a whole, as well as on individual sufferers within it.

Third, in addition to the time and concern which could be given by any person of good will, regardless of religious beliefs or the lack of them, I believe there is a special and distinctive way in which Christian churches can be vehicles of healing. It stems from the fact that we are called to share the resources of the One who showed himself to be "infectious with wholeness" in a unique way. Even doctors who do not share the Christian faith are sometimes moved to acknowledge these resources.

Mildred is a woman who, in her late middle years, began to suffer badly from a distressing and debilitating bowel condition. She consulted a local specialist, who tried various forms of treatment. They all proved ineffective. Finally she came to me to discuss her life and her medical problem, and she attended some healing services at St. Stephen's. I taught her several methods of healing prayer, especially the one which I call "the ring of peace" (described on pp. 71-74 of *How to Pray When Life Hurts*). Her bowel condition responded immediately, and Mildred informed her doctor about her healing and the circumstances which had brought it about.

Soon afterward the vicarage telephone rang. It was Mildred's doctor, confirming the improvement in her condition. I remember his words clearly. He said, "There are two things I want to say to you. First, I see exactly how you have brought about Mildred's cure. Her medical condition was a symptom of an underlying anxiety and lack of self-worth. You have brought her a new security and peace. Her irritable bowel syndrome has responded to that security and peace. The second thing I have to admit is that I was totally unable to produce this effect myself.

She needed your resources, not mine."

This doctor did not profess the Christian faith, but he became a decided enthusiast for the ministry of Christian healing. We spent many hours discussing the issues involved. He told me of his conviction of the existence of a mysterious element in healing which he termed "the X-factor." This X-factor had, he believed, "not a lot to do with conventional medicine but everything to do with what Christians call the Holy Spirit."

It helped our relationship that the doctor believed he could see the psychodynamic background behind a Christian healing. This is not always the case. It was not so in the story which began this chapter. The doctor there could see no medical explanation for the disappearance of what was considered a terminal cancer, but he was still well aware of the "X-factor" power at work.

I should add that, just as there are cases where medical treatment needs to be followed by spiritual treatment before there is a healing result, the opposite can also be true: spiritual treatment often needs to be followed by medical treatment before healing takes place. It is also true, unhappily, that there are many cases in which after both medical and spiritual treatment physical healing does not follow. Healing is a mystery. Churches need to acknowledge this. Doctors need to acknowledge it too.

So where should we go from here—medics, clerics and all who have a concern for the work of healing?

I have no doubt that there is a long journey ahead. I also have no doubt that it will be better if we undertake that journey *together*.

This will require humility. I was very moved when Mildred's doctor said to me during the course of a long discussion one evening, "Your therapeutic armamentarium is greater than mine." Long words and simple humility can go hand in hand!

An occasion also comes to mind when I had been invited to give a public lecture about Christian healing a few miles away from my home, and a local doctor seemed determined to refute everything I had to say. He gave me a hard time. Again and again he stood up and argued against the case I was seeking to make.

However, the next day my telephone rang. It was the same doctor, and he said, "I have been thinking about all you said last night. You were right. I was wrong. Tell me how we can work together." Since then, for a dozen years or so, he and I have run a doctor-clergy group together at the local postgraduate medical center. Such groups can be invaluable, and all sorts of good consequences can flow from them.

The Benefits of Working as a Team

With humility must come greater understanding. Doctor-clergy groups can enable members of both professions to talk together, think together and learn together. We can increasingly penetrate the meaning of one another's vocabulary, and greater understanding can lead to greater trust.

With that greater trust should come greater cooperation. When the healing professions work together, the end result can be remarkable.

In my book *Christian Healing Rediscovered* (Downers Grove, Ill.: InterVarsity Press, 1980, p. 52), I told the story of Betty, a young girl whose quality of life was ruined by recurring vulvitis (inflammation of the genital area). This condition had its roots in a deep anxiety which itself was based on childhood experiences. Betty's quality of life was impaired both physically and mentally, and she saw no way forward into a normal future. Sexuality terrified her. She believed she could never marry and have children. An eminent gynecologist had failed to alleviate her condition in any way. In fact, consultations with him terrified her, and his catheter had begun to acquire a sinister sexual symbolism as far as Betty was concerned. Her family doctor felt helpless. The gynecologist felt angry at her attitude to him. The situation could have ended in total failure, but fortunately it turned into an occasion of interdisciplinary cooperation which was well ahead of its time.

The therapeutic team consisted of the gynecologist, the family doctor, a psychiatrist whom I knew, my wife Eira and me. Each provided part of the jigsaw puzzle.

The gynecologist agreed to see me and described Betty's medical condition in a way I could understand. The family doctor provided important details of Betty's family background. The psychiatrist provided the all-important information that vulvitis can be caused by a condition of deep anxiety. I saw Betty for many hours and sought to immerse her in the knowledge of God's unfailing love in Christ by counseling and prayer. When Betty showed signs of panic about her sexuality, Eira spent time with her, lovingly telling her the relevant facts of life from her experience as a physiotherapist who specialized in antenatal care. When Betty's parents expressed concern that a clergyman was trying to deal with a condition which they considered to be mainly medical, the family doctor reassured them that we were all working as a team.

In a surprisingly short time the condition subsided. I knew Betty was better when one day she said to me, "If it would ever help somebody else to tell them about me, I wouldn't mind."

That was the story as far as it could be told at the time of the previous book. But now, after the passage of time, I can bring it up to date. The improvement in Betty's condition proved to be a lasting one, and in time she fell in love and was married. She is now the mother of a fine son and daughter. Betty has become a prominent local Christian leader. Her daughter has offered herself for ordination, and my guess is that she may well make a notable contribution to the life of the church in the years ahead. Betty knows she owes all of this to the ministry of Christian healing, but none of it could have happened had not five people representing five different healing disciplines decided to work together.

Before ending this chapter, two further points should be made. I believe that those of us who believe in the ministry of Christian healing must be sympathetic to the doubts and fears doctors sometimes display. Doctors may have come across some serious malpractice—perhaps Christian Scientists refusing medical treatment in a way that seems neither Christian nor scientific, or Jehovah's Witnesses refusing to allow a sick child a blood transfusion, or spiritualists offering fraudulent "psychic surgery." Or they may have experienced a Christian healing service conducted in an idiom which they find personally distasteful, and they may not realize that this ministry is not confined to any single idiom but can be offered in terms of any sort of legitimate worship pattern or denominational style.

Our own healing services in Prenton seem now to be widely accepted within medical circles, because it is seen that they are in no way manipulative or exploitative and that nobody is harmed but many claim to be helped. However, this has taken years to achieve. We must be patient.

Last, in this book which seeks to look at many of the instruments or channels of Christian healing, I want to stress that good medical practice can itself be prominent among these channels. If medicine is consciously given or received in the name of Jesus, I believe that a new dimension comes into the treatment and it becomes a specific channel of the healing power of Christ.

I can never be sufficiently grateful for the good, caring medical treatment which at one time or another has been given to my parents, my wife, my children and myself. Often God has blessed it and blessed us through it. There is no discrepancy at all between good medical practice and the healing ministry of Jesus. Often the two can be one.

— FIVE —

RESOURCES
& METHODS

Many years ago, when I was just beginning to think about the ministry of Christian healing, I spent a couple of hours in a car driving George Bennett to a conference. Reverend Bennett was one of the founding fathers of the rediscovered healing ministry in Britain, and his book *The Heart of Healing* is still one of the best primers on Christian healing that I know. For two hours I bombarded him with questions, and patiently and graciously he answered them one by one.

One of my questions was about the resources involved in Christian healing. I remember saying that if I had to visit my doctor, his resources were plain to see. His prescription pad would be at the ready on his desk. His stethoscope might well be around his neck. I knew that behind him were the ranks of specialists with their assorted gadgetry and skills. By contrast, if someone came to me for the ministry of Christian healing, what would my resources be?

George Bennett looked rather surprised and, as if it were the most obvious thing in the world, answered, "Why, God the Father, God the Son and God the Holy Spirit." Of course he was right.

Only One Healer

We have already seen that there is only one "Healer" at a Christian healing service—Jesus himself, who has promised that when two or three are gathered together in his name he will be in the midst (Mt 18:20). When the One who is infectious with wholeness is among us, we should not be surprised if something of his wholeness rubs off on us. Logically, we should be surprised if we are *not* different after encountering his presence.

This thought needs to be set within the context of the Holy Trinity. Jesus is never alone when he is with us. In his own words, "The Father is in me, and I in the Father" (Jn 10:38); "I and the Father are one" (Jn 10:30); "Anyone who has seen me has seen the Father" (Jn 14:9). To worship in the name of Jesus is to make real contact with God the Father, and this contact must in its own right be vibrant with healing. At the beginning of the Bible, in Genesis chapter one, the point is hammered home that creativity is the essence of the Father's nature. Since God is self-consistent (Jas 1:17), when he encounters that which is damaged, his creativity must logically bring a mighty influence for re-creativity (or healing) into any situation where we allow him access. The Lord who "created in the beginning" (see Gen 1:1) is also "the LORD, who heals" (Ex 15:26).

Moreover, in the words of the Nicene Creed, the Holy Spirit "proceeds from the Father and the Son." When a congregation comes together to worship the Father in the name of the Son, the Holy Spirit must be active in the midst both corporately and individually. We are promised that the heavenly Father will "give the Holy Spirit to those who ask him" (Lk 11:13). We have the guarantee of Jesus that the Spirit of truth "will be in you" (Jn 14:17). Jesus actually commands his followers, "Receive the Holy Spirit" (Jn 20:22).

Since, in the words of the Nicene Creed, the Holy Spirit is "the Lord and giver of Life," when he moves among and within us, we should expect him to upgrade our level of life, physically, mentally and spiritually—and, conversely, we should expect him gently (or not so gently) to nudge aside those things in us which are contrary to God's will for our wholeness at every level of life.

So we need hardly fear that the ministry of Christian healing is underresourced if the resources are no less than the presence and power of the Holy Trinity: God the Father, God the Son, God the Holy Spirit.

However, hard on the heels of the question "What are the resources of the ministry of Christian healing?" comes a further question: "What are the ways and means, the channels and outlets through which those healing resources can come into the world today?" It is to that question that we turn during the remainder of this book.

How Do I Fit In?

At this point I have a blockbuster thought for you. You will expect to find details here of means of healing such as the laying on of hands with prayer, anointing with oil, the ministry of deliverance, healing services and Christian counseling. All of these things will follow—and more besides.

However, it may come as a shock to read that according to the Bible, if you are a Christian, your principal channel for the Christian healing ministry is *you*. Members of the Christian church are called not just to *have* channels or to *use* channels, but to *be* channels. (Let me make it clear that being a channel of the Holy Spirit is the exact opposite of New Age "channeling," which consists of opening oneself up as a channel for occult or satanic powers. Christians should use prayer and discernment to stay far away from any such involvement.)

The apostle Paul writes to his fellow Christians, "You are the body of Christ" (1 Cor 12:27). This does not sound particularly startling to our ears because we are used to employing the word *body* in a loose, metaphorical way to denote a group of people, as when an officer inspects a squad of soldiers, finds nothing to complain about and says, "Fine body of men, Sergeant." In Greek this usage is very rare. My classical Greek dictionary provides dozens of examples of the meaning of *soma,* the Greek word for *body.* In all of these I can find only one instance in which it means a group of people. Its normal meaning is a literal, physical body of flesh and bones and organs. My Greek-Cypriot barber tells me that when he speaks Greek today, he still uses the word in the same literal way, and never to mean a group of people.

So when the apostle Paul said that Christians are the "body" of Christ, the word must have had a strange ring in the ears of his contemporaries. It is as though he is claiming a physical identity between us and Jesus. We are to be his arms, his legs, his voice, his heart.

Paul is even capable of using the words *Christ* and *the church* interchangeably. In 1 Corinthians 12:12 he writes, "The body is a unit, though it is made up of many parts; and though all its parts are many, they form one body. So it is with . . ." Can you finish the quotation? We would expect it to end, "So it is with the church," but what Paul actually says is, "So it is with *Christ.*" Martin Luther comments, "He calls Christ the church!"

St. Teresa of Ávila had it right in these famous words: "Christ has no body now on earth but yours, no hands but yours, no feet but yours. Yours are the feet with which he must go about doing good. Yours are the hands with which he must bless men now."

So if you are a Christian, if you have truly invited Jesus Christ into your life to be Savior, Lord and Friend, here is an exercise for you. Put this book down and hold your hands out in front of you. Look at your hands carefully.

Those are the hands of Jesus.

It is a salient thought as we move to the next chapter.

SIX

THE LAYING ON
OF HANDS
WITH PRAYER

*P*rayer is our primary lifeline to God. If God's life is to flow into us and through us into the world, we must be people of prayer.

Christians are accustomed to hearing this sort of thing said, because churches are always telling their members to pray for the world, for society, for the healing of the sick, for the healing of the nations and for the coming of the kingdom of God. However, though we are told we must pray, often this is left as a general exhortation and we are not given detailed instruction about *how* we are to pray.

In my parish we have learned a great deal by sharing in a school of prayer which lasted for two years, during which we came together once a month to learn about healing prayer. Month after month we explored a variety of simple prayer methods. Each method was explained with the help of printed notes. After the explanation, each member of the congregation was given the opportunity to go to a quiet place within the church building and to personally offer the type of prayer that had been taught. Then there was an opportunity to ask questions and share experiences. At the end of the evening the whole congregation was led in a corporate experience of the same prayer method.

Since then it has been my privilege to lead similar schools of prayer in a number of congregations and other groups. InterVarsity Press invited me to write *How to Pray When Life Hurts,* describing some of the prayer methods we have discovered and some of the experiences which have accompanied their use. I will not repeat that material here, but may I suggest you use that book in conjunction with the present chapter.

Two Prayer Methods

The prayer methods fall into two types. In one type the worshiper begins by pondering a basic Christian truth such as the protecting power of the peace of God, or the promise to believers of the presence of Jesus day by day, or the interior healing work of the Holy Spirit, or the many truths contained within the Lord's Prayer or the Apostles' Creed. As we ponder these truths we find ourselves absorbing and channeling their healing implications both for our own benefit and for the benefit of others.

The other type of prayer begins by acknowledging a common experience of life and discovers that in each case there is a way of prayer specifically suitable for that experience. The sort of questions we need to address are as follows.

☐ How do you pray when you feel guilty or ashamed?

☐ How do you pray when you are angry or depressed?

☐ How do you pray when life has hurt you?

☐ How do you pray when you are anxious or fearful?

☐ How do you pray when you are busy and stressed?

☐ How do you pray when you feel jealous or envious?

☐ How do you pray when you or others are ill?

☐ How do you pray when this illness seems not to be getting better?

☐ How do you pray in bereavement?

In all these situations and many more besides it is the will of God to meet us at our point of need through Jesus Christ and to make a healing and life-transforming difference through that meeting.

It is a great joy to me to see the tangible difference participating in a school of prayer can make to people in need. We have already thought about Lydia, who recovered her hearing at a school of healing prayer on the Isle of Man. Jacyntha also comes to mind. She told me that she doubted whether she would be able to take a meaningful part in the school of prayer which she attended, because of the intensity of the arthritic pain she was suffering, but she found that during the course of the evening all her pain was taken from her. At the end of the evening she shared this healing experience with us, and we were all able to thank God for it.

Even more remarkable was the case of Mara, who seemed to undergo a total personality change during a school of healing prayer. Members of her church contacted me afterward to say that this once bitter, awkward, disgruntled woman, whom they had all been tempted to avoid, had overnight become a joy to them all—a reminder that Christian healing is just as much concerned with the mind and the spirit as with the body.

I find it thrilling and humbling that even just reading *How to Pray When Life Hurts* has itself been enough to bring healing to some. Lynne, an editorial assistant who deals with Christian publications, happened to come across the book and then wrote to me to say, "How blessed I was by reading *How to Pray When Life Hurts*, which I obtained from IVP. After following the prayers outlined in your book, I received healing from the Lord for a neck condition and headaches within a few weeks, for which I had been having physiotherapy for two years!"

You could make up your own book of prayers, and in it you could describe prayer methods which have proved helpful and healing to you personally, when life has hurt you or those you love.

For instance, the Ignatian method of prayer involves picturing biblical events in your mind. You experience by imagination the sights, the sounds and the smells in each Bible story. You seek to enter the experience of the people involved on each occasion and may be led to identify yourself with one of them or perhaps to imagine being present in your own right. As in your imagination you encounter Jesus, you seek to listen to his voice and to feel his touch. You bring both yourself and anyone for whom you wish to pray into his presence, so that they may be a gift to him and he may be a gift to them.

If you find this method natural and helpful, you could gradually go through the life of Jesus, starting with the Christmas story and then selecting various events within Jesus' life and ministry—such as, perhaps, the healing of the man on the stretcher who was let down through the roof into the presence of Christ (Mt 9:1-8; Mk 2:1-12; Lk 5:17-25)—and then moving to the events of Holy Week, Good Friday and Easter, and continuing to the remarkable events of Pentecost and Ascension Day.

It may be helpful if I offer you an example. So let's take the occasion in the list above which many find most difficult to picture—the events of Ascension Day. My suggestion is that you now make a prayer-space in your schedule, and try this method for yourself.

Breath of Mountain Air: A Prayer-Meditation on the Ascension

Begin by reading the story of the ascension in Matthew 28:16-20 and Acts 1:6-9.

Picture yourself on the Mount of Ascension with the disciples. If you have never been to Palestine, select a hill you know and love, maybe from your own locality or from a holiday experience. Your own hill will serve the prayer purpose just as well.

As you wait with the disciples, you find your mind goes back to the events leading up to the ascension.

You think back to the pain and the mystery of the crucifixion. Love hangs upon the cross where *our* sins have put him and says, "I'll never give up—and I'll never hit back." Remember the words of Scripture: "He was despised and rejected by men, a man of sorrows, and familiar with suffering. Like one from whom men hide their faces he was despised, and we esteemed him not. Surely he took up our infirmities and carried our sorrows, yet we considered him stricken by God, smitten by him, and afflicted. But he was pierced for our transgressions, he was crushed for our iniquities; the punishment that brought us peace was upon him, and by his wounds we are healed" (Is 53:3-5).

Then you find yourself thinking of the mystery of the resurrection. Love can be put to death but cannot be held by death. Hate, though it kills, has death at its heart and will self-destruct, whereas love, though it dies, has life at its heart and will rise again. So Jesus is alive, and reports of his resurrection have been coming from many sources: from individuals, from small groups, from larger groups and once from a crowd of over five hundred people (1 Cor 15:3-8).

The disciples are bewildered. Some have doubts (Mt 28:17), but discipleship has proved stronger than doubt. Christ has called you all to the Mount of Ascension, and here you are.

Then suddenly Jesus is there with you. He looks glorious. You are moved to worship, as was Thomas when he said the famous words "My Lord and my God!" (Jn 20:28).

Picture the scene. Take your time. As St. Teresa has said, "Hurry is the death of prayer." So stop, look and listen.

Jesus speaks of his *kingship*. "All authority in heaven and on earth has been given to me" (Mt 28:18). Accept his kingship—in your body, your mind, your spirit, your attitudes, your relationships, your lifestyle. Accept his kingship in time and in eternity.

He speaks of his *commissioning* and of your commissioning as well. You are to go into the world for him. You are not only to be a disciple but to make disciples (Mt 28:19). You are to be a channel of his love, his power, his purpose. Accept this commission.

He speaks of his *omnipresence*. Ascension Day is a celebration of the omnipresence of Jesus. During his earthly ministry and even during the forty days after Easter, Jesus was in only one place at a time, but now all restrictions of time and space have been removed. We have his promise, his guarantee: "I am with you always, to the very end of the age" (Mt 28:20). Accept and celebrate his word.

Then, on the peak of the Mount of Ascension, the mist begins to swirl around Jesus. It becomes thicker and thicker until he can no longer be seen. In the traditional terminology of the King James Version, "a cloud received him out of sight" (Acts 1:9). When the mist clears, he is gone—gone to his throne.

Where is his throne? It is in heaven. In the words of the Nicene Creed, "He ascended into Heaven and is seated at the right hand of the Father"—beyond space and time. Attempt the impossible. Picture the cosmic Christ.

His throne is also in the heart of every believer. Once again, reaffirm his enthronement in your own life. As Caroline Maria Noel writes in the hymn "At the Name of Jesus":

In your hearts enthrone Him;
There let Him subdue
All that is not holy,
All that is not true;
Crown Him as your Captain
In temptation's hour,
Let His will enfold you
In its light and pow'r.

Remember you are the subject of the King (Phil 2:10).

Remember you are a soldier of the King (1 Tim 6:12).

Remember you are a member of the Royal Family and share in the

King's authority and power (Rev 1:6).

Absorb a sense of your status and role as you claim and practice his omnipresence. This is a healing experience. Being with Jesus is always so. It is also an empowering one. So bring any to Jesus for whom you wish to pray. Hold them before the cosmic Christ. Hold them before the Christ on the throne of your heart. Remember that he is with you and he is with those for whom you pray. Affirm the holy and healing will of Christ, the ascended and omnipresent King.

Remain in this holy place, breathing in the air on the Mount of Ascension for as long as you wish. Listen for any specific commission which the King may have for you.

Then when the time is right, as you come down from the mountaintop, pray: "Almighty God, through Christ our King I offer you my soul and body. Send me out in the power of your Spirit to live and work to your praise and glory. Amen."

You may need to practice this method of prayer several times before it comes to life for you. I hope that sooner or later it will shine for you with the radiance of Jesus and be an exciting, liberating, therapeutic way of praying. I hope you and those for whom you pray will benefit as you offer it and yourself to God. However, if this prayer method does not work for you, do not worry; Ignatian prayer does not suit everyone. If you are not the Ignatian type, try another form of healing prayer. God is infinite, and the prayer pathways to him are also infinite. It may, for instance, be helpful to try the alternative method of Bible-praying which you will find in chapter eleven.

The Laying On of Hands

This chapter is entitled "The Laying On of Hands with Prayer." So far I have made no reference to the laying on of hands. This has been deliberate, because when hands are laid on a sufferer with prayer in the Christian healing ministry, the prayer is more important than the hands.

However, this does not mean that the laying on of hands is insignificant. It has always had a central place in the ministry of Christian healing, and there are various reasons for this.

Why Lay On Hands?

It is natural to touch those we are seeking to help or comfort. When a little boy falls and scuffs his knee and comes weeping into the kitchen, his mother knows naturally that it is not sufficient to stand at the other end of the room and tell him he will be all right. She instinctively sits him on her knee, gives his leg a rub and says, "It will be better now." And, lo and behold, so it is! There is healing in a loving touch.

Scripture tells us that Jesus incorporated this natural ingredient of human care into the heart of his healing ministry. For instance, after the healing of Peter's mother-in-law, "when the sun was setting, the people brought to Jesus all who had various kinds of sickness, and laying his hands on each one, he healed them" (Lk 4:40).

Jesus expected his followers to incorporate the laying on of hands into the heart of the healing ministry they derived from him. He said, "Those who believe . . . will place their hands on sick people, and they will get well" (Mk 16:17-18). In other words, the Christian church, as the body of Christ, is not only to speak the Word of Christ but also to give the touch of Christ.

It is worth noting that the prerequisite for laying on hands is not ordination to the clerical ministry or the possession of some special gift. It is simple belief—belief in Jesus as Savior and Lord, belief in his healing ministry, belief in the validity of its continuation in his body, the church.

There is no doubt that the laying on of hands goes well with prayer for healing. Often, when I visit someone who is ill, there is no time for the sort of lengthy prayer of which the Ignatian reflection on the ascension is an example. There are just a few minutes available to focus the creativity of God the Father, the healing presence of God the Son and the availability of the Holy Spirit with all his life-giving power on the sick person. So I find myself making the most of the moments available by putting one or both of my hands on the head of the person concerned, and if I have a free hand I use it for a hand clasp. Or possibly (more rarely and only if appropriate) I touch the affected part of the body.

I usually pray spontaneously rather than using a set prayer. I might use such words as these: "Father, let these hands of mine convey the touch of Jesus, the love of Jesus, the healing power of Jesus. John (Mary), I claim all that God has in his generous heart for you here and now. God our Father and Creator re-create you by his mighty power in body, mind and spirit. God the Son, our Lord Jesus Christ, meet you at your point of need and hold you in his strong and loving presence. And the healing influence of God the Holy Spirit, Lord and Giver of life, move within you, freeing you from all that could hurt you and bringing you new life at every level of your being. The blessing of God Almighty, Father, Son and Holy Spirit, rest upon you, surge within you and bring you wholeness, joy and peace. Amen."

The laying on of hands with a shorter prayer is also a key ingredient of the Christian healing services which we hold. There will be full details of these services in chapter nine.

What Can We Expect to Happen?

When Christian prayer and the laying on of hands come together in an act of ministry, either privately or publicly, remarkable things can happen.

Some people experience strange sensations when they lay on hands or have hands laid on them in the name of Jesus. For example, ministrants can sometimes experience tingling or trembling hands. It can be even stranger for recipients. Tess told me that my hands were red hot when I laid hands on her for healing. It was surprising, because my hands are usually distinctly cold—but Tess needed to learn that there was something in her life which God wanted to burn away. Eric experienced what he described as an electric shock when he received the laying on of hands. "How did you do that?" he asked me. Others have experienced tingling sensations or an enhanced sense of light. A few have found themselves falling to the ground when I laid hands on them—rather to my embarrassment!

If there is a purpose in experiences such as these, it may possibly be to encourage our materialistic and sensation-hungry world to take Christian healing seriously. This world likes and perhaps needs visible tokens of power. But I want to put on record my conviction that these phenomena are *not* a guide to whether healing is or is not taking place. I have known startling phenomena to be experienced without any subsequent evidence of healing. On the other hand, I have known many cases where nothing at all was felt during the laying on of hands but startling healings followed.

The young nurse was certainly startled when the dentist to whom I referred in chapter three discovered that his soaring temperature had reverted to normal. "This thermometer is broken," she said. "This temperature can't be right." But it was right, and a second thermometer proved it. I also remember the shock experienced by a senior hospital nurse after I laid hands on and prayed for a woman whom the nurse assured me was "as good as dead," and the almost-corpse sat up and went on to make a totally unexpected recovery. However, in both of these instances the patient did not report feeling anything unusual at the moment of the laying on of hands.

My expectation is that *when there has been prayer with the laying on of hands, whether it has been accompanied by sensations or not, there will always be blessing and strengthening unless the Lord is resisted.* Often the blessing and strengthening will be accompanied by some sort of physical, mental or spiritual healing. This may be either total or partial. In many cases it will be medically explicable, as in the case of Mildred in chapter four. Occasionally it will seem totally inexplicable, and we may find ourselves wondering whether to speak in terms of a miracle. Paradoxically, "results" are often best when our minds are not preoccupied with them and we are not allowing our anxiety to place a barrier between the Lord and our awareness of him.

It is best to keep in mind that the touch of Jesus is to be desired for its own sake, for his own sake, irrespective of any byproducts touch may bring. However, if "Jesus Christ is the same yesterday and today and forever" (Heb 13:8), his touch is never going to be a non-event. When the body of Christ gives the touch of Christ in the context of expectant prayer, a channel of healing is open, and we can leave the rest in the hands of the Lord.

Julia's Story

I have written on this subject at some length, but I would like to tell one further story, because it concerns an event that happened yesterday just as I was finishing this chapter.

Julia, a member of our congregation, suffered a brain hemorrhage ten days ago and had to be rushed to the hospital. The whole congregation covered her with prayer, and the operation seemed to be a success. However, it left her with a throbbing headache which the hospital had no means of alleviating. Yesterday I went in to see her. She was grateful for all that had been done for her, but her face was drawn with the throbbing pain. As I sat by her bed I took one of her hands in both of mine, closed my eyes and began to pray—not concentrating on the throbbing pain which was such a trial to her but affirming the peace and the power and the healing will of God.

When I opened my eyes after five or ten minutes of prayer, I found that Julia had put her other hand on her own head and was sitting with a glowing expression on her face.

"It's gone," she said. "I felt it go, out of my head, through my hand and away." Carefully she put her hand on various parts of her head. With each touch she said, "No throbbing here—no throbbing here—no throbbing here."

As I sat and looked at her, the actual shape of her face seemed to change before my eyes as she smiled and relaxed. Even the postoperative bruising seemed to be healing.

I told her she looked different. She told me she felt different. We sat in silence for a while. God felt very great and I felt very small.

As I left she said four words which I believe I will never forget. She just said, "You are his messenger."

And so can each one of us be.

— S E V E N —

ANOINTING
WITH OIL

*T*he laying on of hands is not the only outward sign associated with healing in the Scriptures or in the early traditions of the Christian church. Another sign or means is that of anointing with oil. This is a common biblical practice and is used for several purposes.

Oil is a sign of commissioning. Prophets, priests and kings were anointed for their work. For instance, in 1 Samuel 10:1, "Samuel took a flask of oil and poured it on Saul's head and kissed him, saying, 'Has not the LORD anointed you leader over his inheritance?' " And in 1 Samuel 16:13, "Samuel took the horn of oil and anointed [David] in the presence of his brothers, and from that day on the Spirit of the LORD came upon David in power."

In a similar way kings and queens of England are anointed for their office by the Archbishop of Canterbury before they are crowned.

Oil is also a sign of honor. The woman who anointed Jesus in Luke

7:36-38 was honoring him. When on the same occasion Simon the Pharisee failed to anoint Jesus, he was withholding honor. Jesus saw the difference and pointed out the contrast (v. 46).

Oil is also a sign of joy. Isaiah 61:3 speaks of "the oil of gladness" and the psalms speak of anointing as a token both of joy and of honor. "You anoint my head with oil; my cup overflows" (Ps 23:5). "God, your God, has set you above your companions by anointing you with the oil of joy" (Ps 45:7). "How good and pleasant it is when brothers live together in unity! It is like precious oil poured on the head, running down on the beard, running down on Aaron's beard, down upon the collar of his robes" (Ps 133:1-2). In our ears this is hardly an attractive picture, but for the psalmist it evoked pure delight!

Above all, for Christians oil is a sign of unity with Jesus Christ. The name Jesus means "Savior." The title Christ means "anointed." Jesus Christ is the one who has been anointed to be Savior of the world. When we call ourselves "Christians" ("anointed ones") we are affirming our oneness with the anointed Savior.

Because of all these nuances, anointing is a fitting symbol and channel within the Christian healing ministry.

Where Anointing Started

Anointing was actually a medical procedure in its own right in the ancient world. Isaiah compares sinful Israel to a senseless person whose body is injured and festering but who rejects all medication. The list of medical procedures includes anointing with oil. Addressing Israel he writes, "From the sole of your foot to the top of your head there is no soundness—only wounds and welts and open sores, not cleansed or bandaged or soothed with oil" (Is 1:6). In Jesus' parable of the good Samaritan, when the traveler had been beaten, stripped and left half-dead by robbers, the Samaritan "went to him and bandaged his wounds, pouring on oil and wine" (Lk 10:34)—wine as a disinfectant and oil to help the healing process.

The New Testament tells us that the Christian church incorporated the practice of anointing into its healing ministry. The disciples used it. They "anointed many sick people with oil and healed them" (Mk 6:13). It became part of the ministry of the elders in congregations of the early church. James writes, "Is any one of you in trouble? He should pray. Is anyone happy? Let him sing songs of praise. Is any one of you sick? He should call the elders of the church to pray over him and anoint him with oil in the name of the Lord. And the prayer offered in faith will make the sick person well; the Lord will raise him up. If he has sinned, he will be forgiven. Therefore confess your sins to each other and pray for each other so that you may be healed" (Jas 5:13-16).

It is not altogether clear whether these texts refer to symbolic acts of spiritual healing or whether they just represent the provision of basic medical care. However, it is indisputable that very soon the Christian church saw in the act of anointing a powerful channel of the healing power of Christ. The Apostolic Tradition of Hippolytus (c. A.D. 170-236) contains this prayer for the blessing of oil: "Send, O Lord, your Spirit upon this oil, by which you have anointed priests, kings and prophets, that it may give health to body, soul and spirit."

There are references to anointing as a channel of Christian healing in the Didache (a manual of Christian morality and worship which may be from as early as the first century A.D.), in the apocryphal Acts of Thomas (from the early third century) and in the earliest Roman missals, the Gelasian and Gregorian sacramentaries.

Innocent I (who was Pope from 402 to 417) wrote, "The faithful who are sick can be anointed with holy oil, which has been prepared by the Bishop and which not only priests but all the faithful may use for anointing."

Alcuin's Rite of Anointing (c. 735-804) contains the prayer "Through the anointing of consecrated oil and our prayers, cured and warmed by the Holy Spirit, may you merit to receive your former health and even better health."

However, by the time of Thomas Aquinas (1225-1274) we notice a change. The purpose of anointing was now seen as a preparation for death. Peter Lombard (c. 1100-1160) wrote, "Unction prepares those who are departing this world for the divine vision," and anointing became known as "extreme unction."

This was properly rejected at the Reformation as being unscriptural, but in rejecting the whole practice of anointing, Reformers threw out the baby with the bath water! It is right that the church as a whole is now tending to go back to the earlier practice.

In my own ministry, the occasions when I have anointed the sick have been relatively infrequent compared with the many times when I have laid on hands with prayer. I suppose the reason for this is that I do not carry oil around as I visit my parish, but I always have my hands with me! From a purely practical point of view, it is easier to offer a laying on of hands than to anoint. However, sometimes anointing seems to be the more appropriate form of ministry, particularly if hands have been laid on with prayer on several occasions without any noticeable evidence of healing, or if a deep and serious condition seems to suggest that the solemn symbolism involved in anointing is particularly fitting— or if anointing is specifically requested.

How to Anoint

It may be helpful to offer some practical hints on procedures at this point, so here are some suggestions—many of them based on the practice of George Bennett, about whom I wrote in chapter five.

Where possible it is advisable to make a preparatory visit in order to explain something of the origin, the meaning and the biblical background of anointing. The sufferer should be given the option of accepting or declining this ministry, and it should be made clear that anointing is in no way a magic act. Before leaving it is helpful to suggest prayers which the sufferer may wish to use and Bible passages (like the story of the good Samaritan in Luke 7 and the advice about the healing ministry in James 5:13-16) which should be read and absorbed as a preparation for the day of anointing.

On the day of the anointing, it is important to make sure that there is plenty of time available. This ministry requires an unhurried opportunity for sharing a time of stillness, for practicing the presence of God, for affirming his healing will and for asking for an openness to all that God may wish to do.

Many Church of England clergy choose to use oil that has been blessed by a bishop, but this is optional. Whether it has been blessed or not, the oil should be offered afresh to God at every anointing that it may be used as his symbol, his channel. Remembering the teaching of James, who links anointing with the confession of sins, the question should be asked, "Is there anything you wish to tell me about your life?" Any response must be sensitively dealt with and met with the resources of the gospel.

A Bible passage should be read—either one of those which has already been mentioned, or verses from Psalms 46, 91 or 121, or perhaps Isaiah 35:3-6 or 40:27-31, or the closing verses of Romans 8, or Luke 11:9-13, or some other passage which strikes you as suitable for the person to whom you are ministering. First names should be used throughout the act of anointing: "John (Mary), I come to you in the name of Jesus, your Savior, your Friend, the Son of God, the Lord of Healing." Dip your thumb in the oil and shake off any surplus oil. Or use a container broad-mouthed enough to take a cotton ball, and saturate the cotton ball with oil, so that when you press your thumb into it, your thumb is coated with just the right amount of oil (a method favored by Bishop Morris Maddocks).

Anoint the sufferer on the forehead. I like to make the sign of the cross as I do so, in much the same way as I do at a baptism service. Sometimes it also seems right to anoint the palms of the hands. Words can be used such as "John (Mary), for your healing and for your joy I anoint you with oil in the name of the Father and of the Son and of the Holy Spirit."

Allow the oil to sink in and the significance of the oil to sink in also. George Bennett used to recommend a lengthy time of silent prayer at this point—perhaps as long as half an hour!—before the time of anointing comes to an end with a blessing.

An alternative procedure is to set the anointing within the context of a Communion service, so that the climax of the occasion comes not with the moment of anointing but with the reception of the bread and wine and the act of union with Jesus which this signifies.

Sometimes there is an emergency situation which does not permit either of these lengthy sequences. Spiritual healing, like medical healing, sometimes requires improvisation. The power of God is not diminished on these occasions.

Roger's Story

One of our most notable occasions of anointing happened when a local hospital phoned the vicarage to say that Roger, one of our congregation, was dying. We were told that he could not have more than an hour or two to live at most.

He had been a sick man for years. Now it seemed that he had come to the end of his life on earth. He was in a private room, wired to various sorts of medical gadgets which monitored his condition and showed that many of his vital functions were stopping or had stopped.

I was out and could not be reached, but my wife phoned one of our curates, and he rushed to the hospital, anointed Roger and gave him Holy Communion.

As Roger was anointed for healing in the name of Jesus, unaccountably the medical gadgetry around him showed that his vital functions were returning to working order. The nurses were amazed as they watched the screen beside his bed record the healing process.

Roger went on to live for a further six years—and they were a remarkable six years. There are further details of his story in *How to Pray When Life Hurts* (pp. 88-90).

The experience when the monitoring equipment registered the moment of Roger's healing seemed like pure magic—but it wasn't, and this may well be the right moment to introduce a "failure story" to make certain I am not conveying the wrong message in this chapter.

A Different Result

Fergus was a lovely lad in his early teens—cheerful, courteous, intelligent, good-looking—but he was in a wheelchair, because he was suffering from muscular dystrophy. He was expected to die within a few years because muscular dystrophy normally cripples and kills boys who inherit it. His parents were magnificent in their care and love, but understandably they did not find that Christian faith came easily to them under these conditions, and sometimes it was very clear that there was real anger in them as they watched their son's suffering.

I used to visit the family, and I would tell them some of the funny things which continually happen in parish life. They needed a good laugh and were very willing to have one with me.

Before long I felt moved to lay hands on Fergus and to pray that the healing power of the Holy Spirit would be in him. However, steadily and inexorably he deteriorated. I offered him the ministry of anointing, and happily he accepted. I hardly remember how Fergus and his parents reacted, but I know it was an experience that almost reduced me to tears.

Spiritually Fergus was growing and glowing. I prepared him for confirmation, and he accepted Jesus as his personal Savior, Lord and Friend.

It was a privilege to visit him; I used to feel better for it each time I went. His parents paid for a ramp to be installed at the rear entrance of our church so that Fergus could drive his electric wheelchair to church Sunday by Sunday. We loved having him with us, and all benefited from his membership at St. Stephen's.

However, though his spirit was strong, his body grew weaker month by month, and ultimately he died, still a teenager.

His parents were shattered—as we all were. They moved out of our district to North Wales. I wondered whether they would ever be able to go to church again. I could not have blamed them if anger and pain were to keep them away.

Two years later, unexpectedly I received a letter from Fergus's mother, Morag. She wrote,

Dear Roy,

I have been thinking about you and Eira all week and do hope you are both well. The reason you have been in my thoughts was that I woke up on Monday morning dreaming about you—very vividly for it to remain in my memory! The thing that impressed me very much was your lovely sense of humor. I've never stopped to consider it before, but the dream brought it home to me. Do you yourself realize what a lovely gift God has given you? I bet you have seldom appreciated what a good feeling you have given people by your appreciation of the humor in a situation.

We've all settled down well here. I feel I'm becoming a real person again bit by bit and can now look back a bit and even ahead a bit with hope. I have started to attend the English Presbyterian church.

God be thanked for all your love and goodness to Fergus and to us all.

Morag

Fergus's mother is now working as the chairman of her local Muscular Dystrophy Society. And she is encouraging the people of her new church to develop the ministry of Christian healing.

I have no doubt that spiritually Fergus had a high degree of wholeness when he died and that he was well prepared for the adventure of eternity. It is also good to know that his mother has found a new wholeness in her new life. Possibly this is not such a "failure story" in spite of Fergus's death and all the pain and grief involved.

But why, when Roger's anointing brought such tangible physical results, were there no such results for Fergus?

I would not be honest if I did not pose the question to you, to myself and to God. Later in this book (in chapter twelve) we shall see whether it is possible for us to stumble toward an answer.

EIGHT

THE MINISTRY
OF DELIVERANCE

We saw in the last chapter that, medically speaking, olive oil can be a useful commodity because it can soften scabs and can have a soothing effect if we are hurt and sore. However, in medical treatment very often a condition requires more than softening and soothing. Often when we are ill some unhelpful ingredient has found its way into our bodies and we need to be rid of it in order to be whole again. Soothing ointment will do us no good. We need the surgeon's knife or some other method of getting rid of whatever is damaging us.

Here, as so often is the case, medical care provides a parallel for spiritual care. In the Gospels and the Acts of the Apostles there are over a hundred accounts of healing. Over a third of them involve an element of exorcism or deliverance. An alien influence has to be dispatched in some way.

Some readers may become rather nervous at this point and may be tempted either to omit this chapter or to read it only as a matter of curiosity, bypassing its practical consequences. If you are beginning to have any such feelings I would encourage you to stay with me here, because for my part I find the conclusions of this chapter to be compelling, whether I view them from the standpoint of Scripture, logic or experience.

It is a matter of simple fact that when life goes wrong and we become unhappy, unhealthy and confused, often something has wormed its way into us which should not be there, something that is definitely not part of God's blueprint for us. It might, for instance, be a spirit of fear or of hate or of lust. We may know that it is an "alien ingredient." We may know that it is doing us no good at all in body, mind or spirit, but it may have its hooks well and truly into us and we may not know how to get rid of it in our own strength. If Christ is to make a healing difference to us, he will have to deal with it.

Where do they come from, these alien ingredients which can damage us at so many levels of our being? I believe the Book of Common Prayer points to the right answer when it names the three traditional sources of trouble in our life and experience as "the world, the flesh and the devil." The prayerbook litany offers this simple prayer for use when we are harassed by any or all of these trouble-sources: "From all deceits of the world, the flesh and the devil, Good Lord, deliver us." The compilers of the Church of England's new Alternative Service Book have had the sense not to change or omit this prayer for deliverance.

It is worth looking at each of these trouble-sources in turn.

A World Gone Wrong

The world was created by God and is beloved by God (Jn 3:16), but it has gone wrong and has become enemy-occupied territory (1 Jn 5:17). Many Christians have been called to fight against the world. Some have managed to be strengthened rather than damaged in the process. Some time ago I was privileged to spend an evening with Richard Wurmbrand, who for fourteen years suffered the worst the world could do to him in Rumanian communist prisons. He tells the story in his great book *In God's Underground* (which should, I believe, be compulsory reading for all Christians today!). I was amazed at how, both in this book and in face-to-face contact, he seems to be unscathed by the battles he has fought.

By contrast, many ordinary Christians find that if they are required to do battle in some way with the world they can be damaged in the process. Sometimes the world can leave a visiting card in the deep recesses of the personalities of those who have come into conflict with it. I think of Priscella, an elderly lady whose house was burglarized three times in succession and who was left with a spirit of fear that dominated and debilitated her life. That "spirit of fear" came from the world—or our local part of it, where violent robbery is all too common. She had to leave us for a quiet village in the South of England where the villagers can still leave their doors unlocked and life is tranquil and safe. Because "perfect love drives out fear" (1 Jn 4:18), she needed love and security in order to become whole again.

I understand how she felt, because I was left with a spirit of fear myself after suffering bullying as a schoolboy. In my case, subsequently I found the healing power of the perfect love which drives out fear in Jesus himself.

Human Nature Gone Wrong

The flesh is the biblical term for human nature gone wrong. Paul writes, "I know that nothing good lives in me, that is, in my sinful nature [literally, "my flesh"]. For I have the desire to do what is good, but I cannot carry it out. For what I do is not the good I want to do; no, the evil I do not want to do—this I keep on doing. Now if I do what I do not want to do, it is no longer I who do it, but it is sin living in me that does it. So I find this law at work: When I want to do good, evil is right there with me. For in my inner being I delight in God's law; but I see another law at work in the members of my body, waging war against the law of my mind and making me a prisoner of the law of sin within my members. What a wretched man I am! Who will rescue me from this body of death?" (Rom 7:18-24).

We sometimes use the term "besetting sins" to describe undesirable practices and thought patterns which have locked in on our lives. What seems to happen is that our sinful human nature is tempted by and succumbs to something which, though harmful, appears attractive. We toy with it and give it a place in our pattern of life and thought. Then we are surprised to find that the "besetting sin" is toying with us! It is in charge—and soon the term *toying* becomes totally inappropriate. We have become the prisoner of our besetting sin.

Bridget, a lovely old Irish nun, comes to mind. She told me that as a child she indulged in the luxury of negative thoughts about Protestants. These thoughts rather pleased her, because she and her family suffered real mistreatment at Protestant hands. Gradually the negative thoughts turned into a spirit of hatred. As a nun she knew that this spirit should have no place in her, but it was in charge. It had become her besetting sin. It was poisoning her and she felt powerless to stem the flow of poison.

Patrick also comes to mind—a fine Christian man, but whose life was ruined by a spirit of pornographic lust. His preoccupation with pornography had started as a so-called "fun-practice," but soon it was far from being fun. It was an addiction. He found himself slinking in and out of sex shops, ashamed but unable to resist the compulsion.

I am pleased to tell you that both of these stories have happy endings. Bridget attended an interdenominational worship meeting, confessed her spirit of hate to the people around her and found that, after deliverance prayers, she was totally liberated. She glowed as she subsequently told me the story. I was privileged to minister to Patrick myself and to see the living Lord Jesus deliver him from his addiction and launch him into a new life of Christian freedom, Christian service and Christian joy.

Paul found a similar freedom and healing in Christ. He ends the agonizing verses quoted above by answering his own question: "Who will rescue me from this body of death? Thanks be to God—through Jesus Christ our Lord!" (Rom 7:24-25).

The Enemy and His Agents

The devil (as if the world and the flesh were not enough for us to be struggling with) is a further trouble-source. The Bible teaches that we are not the only created beings in the universe. Nor are we the only beings to have fallen away from our Creator's purpose. Scripture teaches that there is a powerful spiritual being, created by God but in rebellion against God. He is the enemy of the human race (Job 1:6-12). He was the enemy of Jesus during his earthly ministry (Mt 4:1-11). Unlike God, who is omnipresent, Satan can be in only one place at a time. But to some extent he can compensate for this because, according to Scripture, he has a sort of mafia of lesser spirits who share his rebellion against God and who work with him (Rev 12:7-9). His mafia targets the human race and likes to have Christians in its sights (Eph 6:12). Some Christians are deceived (1 Tim 4:1). All Christians are to be on their guard (1 Cor 10:20).

Some interpreters regard all of this as figurative or metaphorical language, a series of pictures to help us understand the reality and danger of evil. Others take the Bible teaching literally and believe in an actual devil and actual demons. Others seem to take a halfway position. They believe in a literal devil but only in figurative demons. I can understand those who take the totally figurative position and those who take the totally literal position, but not those who occupy the halfway house.

They seem to me to be occupying the theologically heretical ground of attributing omnipresence to the devil, and thereby making him much more important than he is.

To put my own cards on the table, I have come over the years to accept the devil and his demons as actual spiritual beings. It is the most straightforward interpretation of Scripture. It matches much pastoral experience. Above all, there seems no doubt that Jesus took Satan and the demonic world seriously and literally. Chapters 8 to 10 of Luke provide several examples.

If you and I face the possibility of unwelcome intruders—a legacy from the world, some aspect of the flesh which has gotten out of control, or unwelcome attention from one of the devil's minions—how are we to deal with the situation in ourselves? And how are we to help others who may come to us for help?

I freely admit that I am a nonspecialist in these spheres, but for what it may be worth, here is a list of some of the principles and practicalities of deliverance, so far as I understand them, and so far as they apply to ordinary ministry.

Principles of Deliverance

First, when considering an alien ingredient or influence in our own or someone else's life, it makes sense to begin by considering the world and the flesh as possible trouble-sources, rather than leaping to a demonic interpretation.

It is possible to become obsessed with the demonic. I was talking to a well-known exorcist some time ago. He had slipped and twisted his ankle. When he told the story, the words he used were "A demon cast me down!" Well, maybe a demon did, but it does seem a complicated explanation for what could be a simple accident.

My feeling is that no good comes from an excessive preoccupation with the devil and his works. Even in the unlikely event of the air around us being thick with demons, Martin Luther reminds us that they should not be our preoccupation.

And were this world all devils o'er,
And watching to devour us,
We lay it not to heart so sore;
Not they can overpower us.
And let the prince of ill
Look grim as e'er he will,
He harms us not a whit;
For why?—his doom is writ;
A word shall quickly slay him.
("A Mighty Fortress Is Our God")

That "word," Luther explains, is "God's word," the only word that ultimately counts. I am reminded of some ancient words of Aurelius Clemens Prudentius (born in A.D. 348):

Ye clouds and darkness, hosts of night,
That breed confusion and affright,
Begone! O'erhead the dawn shines clear,
The light breaks in and Christ is here.

For every occasion on which we direct our ears and eyes to the world of darkness, we should direct them a hundred times to the world of light, to the revelation of God in Christ. That is the Christian perspective.

Second, having established that we should look to the world and the flesh as potential sources for alien influence before we look to the devil, and that even if we have ultimately to turn our thoughts to the devil we do not need to be dismayed, we must make sure we know the reason for this optimistic stance.

It lies simply in the basic Christian conviction that Jesus can cope with the worst that the world, the flesh and the devil can throw at us. While our trust is in him, nothing can separate us from his love and power. "In all these things we are more than conquerors through him who loved us. For I am convinced that neither death nor life, neither angels nor demons, neither the present nor the future, nor any powers, neither height nor depth, nor anything else in all creation, will be able to separate us from the love of God that is in Christ Jesus our Lord" (Rom 8:37-39).

Third, there is more good news. Expert diagnostic powers are not a prerequisite for involvement in the deliverance ministry. Often I find that I do not know, in a certain case, whether a malign influence comes from the world, the flesh or the devil. But I have learned that I do not have to know. It is enough that Christ knows!

Steps You Can Take

I turn now from principles to practicalities.

1. So that we shall not be like the Pharisee who tries to get a splinter out of someone else's eye while ignoring the plank sticking out of his own eye (Mt 7:3-5), the best place to start an involvement in the deliverance ministry is by looking inward. This is the moment to ask the uncomfortable question, *Is there something in me which has no rightful place in me?* If so, you may have an instinct whether it comes from the world, the flesh or the devil—or you may not. In either case, if you place your "plank" in the hands of Jesus, he is well able to remove it. It may involve pain, but it will be good pain—followed by new dimensions of life. The Lord's pain is always better than the devil's pat on the head. All you have to do is to pray the Lord's Prayer ("Deliver us from evil")— and mean it. He will do the rest. He may deliver swiftly. He may deliver gradually. But his power to do so is inexorable if you set it in motion.

2. If you are not resisting the Lord's power of deliverance for yourself, you may well find that he commissions you to be its channel to others. It is important to accept in principle that this ministry has an integral part in Christian healing. You need not actively seek involvement in it, but if it comes along there is no need to be fearful.

3. The opportunity and challenge to exercise this ministry may come in various ways. Sometimes it may be asked for by a sufferer ("I don't know what has got into me. Can you help?") or by someone close to the sufferer. Sometimes it may be a response to a discerned need. Sometimes you may just play a hunch. You may be praying with somebody and unexpectedly find yourself not speaking to God, but in God's name addressing whatever may be damaging or diminishing the person to whom you are ministering.

4. Unless you find yourself unexpectedly caught up in the deliverance ministry in this way, careful preparation is desirable on each occasion. It is good to find out the facts. Take a case history. Gently establish whether there is a medical dimension and whether medication is being taken. If so, you may need to ask a medical colleague whether the condition or the prescribed drug could be responsible for any presenting symptoms. If there is no apparent medical cause, try to identify the psychological or spiritual source of the troublesome element in the sufferer's life. You may, for example, discover some degree of involvement in the occult. However, if you cannot find a source, rest in the fact that Jesus knows the whole situation.

5. If possible before ministry, seek the support of the faith and prayer of others. There should be at least one other person of spiritual maturity with you when the act of ministry takes place.

6. Begin the act of ministry by reading an appropriate Bible passage—perhaps a selection of verses from Romans 7—8, or verses from the Sermon on the Mount (Mt 5—7). Assert the power of Jesus, remembering that "God exalted him to the highest place and gave him the name that is above every name, that at the name of Jesus every knee should bow, in heaven and on earth and under the earth, and every tongue confess that Jesus Christ is Lord, to the glory of God the Father" (Phil 2:9-11). Claim that power for the weakening of whatever may be the root of the problem.

7. When you sense the moment is right, quietly and confidently address the trouble-source (not the Lord or the person afflicted) with words such as these: "In the name of Jesus and by the power of his blood, I rebuke you—spirit of fear [or hate, lust or whatever]—I claim Christ's authority over you and cast you out. Go from this child of God and trouble him [her] no more. Go in the name of the Father. Go in the name of the Son. Go in the name of the Holy Spirit. Go and never return. Amen." If you are not certain what you are dealing with, modify your words: "Whatever it is that troubles you, I command it to leave you. I claim authority by the name of Jesus. Whatever you are, go. Go and trouble this child of God no more." It is my conviction that in nonspecialist deliverance ministry there is no need to augment these simple prayers either by bell, book, candle, salt, water and Latin prayers on the one hand or by lengthy and sensational charismatic procedures on the other.

8. Allow time for the deliverance prayer to sink in. There may or may not be some form of physical reaction. As in the case of other forms of the healing ministry, do not concentrate on the presence or absence of a reaction. Concentrate on the Lord, and now pray directly to him and lay on hands for healing protection and peace.

9. Again allow time for reflection and resting, and before you go recommend constant contact with holy things (e.g., regular and frequent Communion).

10. During the days which follow, keep the sufferer in your prayers. A further visit on the fourth day could be useful. It is sometimes thought that the fourth day may bring a crisis of some sort—as can also be the case after a physical operation.

Getting Outside Help

If you feel you are getting out of your depth at any point, ask for help. You will already have the help of praying friends, but you may also need the help of a reputable trained exorcist. In the Church of England specially trained diocesan exorcists are always available, and other Christian denominations make similar provision. You may need to go back on more than one occasion to consult medical colleagues for their advice. The deliverance ministry often requires the sort of cooperation described in chapter four.

Some would say deliverance ministry should *never* be undertaken without medical and psychiatric cross-checks and even so only by highly trained specialist exorcists. My own conviction is that a sensible, scriptural, low-key deliverance ministry may be required of any believer.

A couple of further illustrations may help you to judge this matter for yourself.

In my earlier book *Christian Healing Rediscovered,* I told the story of two teenagers, Franchette and Josephine. They had become mixed up in a circle which dabbled in the occult, and Franchette had become an exceedingly troubled person. She said that everywhere she went she was dogged by the sense of an evil presence. Josephine was almost equally worried because she could see the effect the "presence" was having on her friend. They had severed their occult connection, but the presence persisted. They asked if I could help. We went into church together. The girls knelt at the Communion rail and I stood behind it. I gave Franchette a crucifix to hold, to concentrate her thoughts, and prayed not in any set form but as the words came, thanking God for his goodness and power and for making that goodness and power available to us. I claimed that power to banish whatever was troubling Franchette, and as we prayed Franchette said, "It has gone."

Josephine subsequently wrote to me to say that Franchette was now completely normal again, and there the story ended, as it was told in my earlier book.

I can now tell you that many years later Josephine wrote again to say that this incident had been the start of a process which led her to personally invite Jesus to be her Savior and Lord. She is now a deeply committed Christian, a pillar of her local church and a new person.

None of this would have happened if I had sent them away because I did not have a psychiatric report and a professional exorcist was not available.

Broderick was a fine Christian man, a leader in his local church, but he was depressed—and there was something strange about his depression. His family asked if I would visit him. I did so several times, but nothing seemed to help. I do have some training in psychotherapy, and so I was able to take a case history and offer him counseling, but it made no difference. He appreciated gentle pastoral contact but seemed no better for it. We prayed together regularly. I took him Holy Communion, but he remained depressed. His doctor was also visiting him regularly and tried out a variety of treatments. They were all of no avail.

Then one day while praying with him, rather to my surprise I found myself going into a deliverance mode of prayer. I found myself addressing whatever it was that was troubling him, taking authority over it in the name of Jesus and ordering it out of him. There was an immediate reaction on Broderick's part, even though I offered no explanation of what I was doing. Within a short time his depression lifted and left. If I had held back on deliverance ministry because I am not a professional exorcist, who can say when and whether healing would have come to him.

To summarize my own ground rules: I believe I must exhaust all other possibilities before I posit the demonic. I must never seek involvement in the world of spirits, but if I just happen to become involved during the course of pastoral care, I need not fear. I must put on the armor of God (Eph 6:11-17), gather prayer support, avail myself of the best advice available and then go, affirming the lordship of Christ, and in his name banish anything that is alien to that lordship.

Of course prevention is better than cure, and how better could this chapter end than with another quotation from the Book of Common Prayer, which reminds that if we allow the purity of Jesus to have access to the depths of our being it will form a barrier against any incursion which the world, the flesh or the devil may make against us. This collect is set for the second Sunday in Lent in the Alternative Service Book and for the eighteenth Sunday after Trinity in the Book of Common Prayer:

Lord God Almighty, grant your people grace to withstand the temptations of the world, the flesh and the devil, and with pure hearts and minds to follow you, the only God: through Jesus Christ our Lord. Amen.

NINE

THE HEALING
POWER
OF WORSHIP

Adrienne is a writer. Some time ago she had a problem. It was a cumbersome wart on one hand which made it difficult for her to write or type. Not only was it a nuisance but it was interfering with her livelihood.

One Sunday, quite unexpectedly, as Adrienne received the bread and wine at our Communion service, the wart dropped off her hand. There was no mark. It was as if the wart had never existed.

Adrienne was delighted, but she thought I might be embarrassed. "Fancy it happening at a service that was not a healing service!" she said. I had to explain to her that there is no such thing as a nonhealing service.

When Jesus Is Present
In our churches we need to rediscover the concept of the healing power

of *all* worship. Christian worship is a meeting with the risen Lord (Mt 18:20). It should never be a nonevent, and we should never be surprised if Jesus makes a tangible difference to us when we come together to practice his presence.

Holy Communion is a healing activity in its own right. Some take the view that it is *the* supreme Christian healing activity. Think of the healing themes which characterize this service. In every Christian denomination, Communion begins with a time of preparation in which we pray that God will make us ready, cleansing our thoughts by the Holy Spirit. Then we wait upon the Word of God as Scripture is read and expounded. We make an affirmation of faith and offer prayers of intercession. We hear afresh a statement of God's saving love, and this gives us the courage to make an act of confession. We hear the words of forgiveness which lie at the heart of the gospel and share a sign of God's peace.

All of this has a power for healing built into it, and this healing power is then focused and intensified through the mysterious act which brings us to the fourfold core and climax of Communion. In the words of Paul (italics mine),

1. The Lord Jesus, on the night he was betrayed, *took* bread,

2. and when he had *given thanks,*

3. he *broke it and said,*

4. "This is my body, which is for you; *do this* in remembrance of me." (1 Cor 11:23-24)

The mystery of the body of Christ reminds us that Christians are those who *take* the Lord Jesus as Savior; we *give thanks* for all he is and all he does; we remember with sorrow that it is our sins that have *broken* him; and as we obey his command to *"do this,"* we find it is all "for us." We both receive and share him.

The mystery deepens as we realize that Christians are not only called to receive, but actually to *be* the body of Christ (1 Cor 12:27); that *we* are privileged to be *taken* into his service; that he *gives thanks* for us and we must be thankful for all we can be in Christ and for each other; that we too are called to experience *brokenness* in order that in *doing this* our own healing and the healing of the world may be furthered.

How much there is to ponder here, and how little we sometimes ponder it. How much there is to receive here, and how little we sometimes receive it. How much there is to share here, and how little we sometimes share it.

As we touch the heart of Holy Communion, we touch the heart of Jesus, and we touch the heart of Christian healing both for ourselves and for others.

We should expect greater things than the dropping off of Adrienne's wart to proceed from such a sacrament!

Every occasion when we come together for Christian worship must be redolent with healing—providing it is real worship, a real meeting with the real Christ.

Even at a Funeral
Funeral services can provide another example.

Most clergy spend a surprisingly large amount of time conducting funeral services. At this moment I am preparing two such services. One is for a seventy-two-year-old man who may well have pined to death. He was completely deaf, but he had a close and happy marriage, and his wife served as his "ears" and enabled him to live a full life. Two years ago she died. He was desolate. His doctor said he was in sound health, and yet he started to reproduce the symptoms which his wife had shown, until he died for no apparent medical reason. The other funeral is for a premature, stillborn baby boy. I have just spent time with his mother. She is unmarried. Her own mother will not speak to her, and her father is dead. Although I do not in any way condone extramarital sexual intercourse, my heart went out to her as we sat in her little flat looking together at photographs of her tiny stillborn baby.

Neither of these funerals is likely to be a large affair. There may be no more than a handful of people at either of them. But the need for healing will be great at both.

What are the ingredients of a healing funeral? I believe there must be an affirmation of the one who has died, but it must not be false or fulsome or isolated from the proclamation of the gospel. If it is false, then the whole service will be devalued. If it is fulsome and is not set firmly within the context of the gospel, then even if its contents are true, people will simply say to themselves, "This was a fine man (woman), and he (she) has gone." They will go out depressed and unhealed.

If there is to be healing, the main ingredient of the service has to be a sensitive presentation of the Christian gospel of resurrection. The service has to deal with the issues which will be in the minds of the mourners. Why do Christians believe there is life after death? What do Christians believe it will be like? Is the resurrection of Jesus a fact or a fairy tale? Can Jesus help us face life and death? What is the Christian hope? How does it affect the way in which we face bereavement? How can it affect life after bereavement? What does it have to say about our own prospect of eternal life?

If these questions are faced and an answer is offered gently and clearly, without evasion but without manipulation (because to manipulate a mourner in a state of grief is unforgivable), then that loveliest of healing phenomena may take place. Someone present may be spiritually awakened, and, paradoxically, new life will begin at a funeral.

Just two weeks ago a woman came up to me at the end of a funeral and said, "It's true, all you have told us about new life starting at a funeral. When my husband's father died, the vicar said much the same thing, and when we were back home my husband started to think about the Christian faith as he had never done before. Eventually he was confirmed and joined our local church. Now he's a committed Christian—and it all started at his dad's funeral."

Christian healing can take place—and should be expected to take place—at Christian funerals, at weddings and baptisms, at ordinary Sunday services, at mission services, at church retreats, in fact on any occasion when Christians come together to practice the presence of God and to ask for his blessing in the name of Jesus Christ.

Special Services

However, along with the other occasions of worship, there is still a significant role for what are known as "Christian healing services," and it would be wrong to end this chapter without saying something about them.

My own conviction is that every church should hold a Sunday healing service once a month. Perhaps it is more than a coincidence that the tree of life with its leaves of healing in the last chapter of the book of Revelation yields fruit twelve times a year!

The format of these services will differ from church to church and from denomination to denomination but should, I believe, be kept similar to the normal pattern of worship in each church, in order to emphasize the healing potential of all worship.

The Three Ingredients

Whatever format is used, it is generally thought that three ingredients have a central place at the heart of a Christian healing service. The first is *the proclamation of the Word of God.* If spiritual healing is to be specifically Christian, it is essential that the simplicities of the gospel are clearly presented at healing services.

The best way I know of doing this is that the first five or six healing services which are held in any church should feature a course of sermons presenting the basic principles of Christian healing, but that when this course is complete, subsequent sermons should consist of a long-term Bible study project. I recommend preaching the whole way through one of the Gospels, month by month, leaving nothing out.

When I do this in my own parish, my aim is first to see the real Jesus for myself as the Gospels present him, and then to communicate that reality simply and clearly. He will do the rest. Subsequently, other New Testament books may also be used for the same purpose. During my many years of ministry at St Stephen's, I have preached my way through Luke's Gospel, the Acts of the Apostles, the first and second letters to the Corinthians, and am now preaching through Matthew's Gospel. Also I have preached through Mark's Gospel and am now preaching John's Gospel at our daughter church. I find the topic presented by each Bible passage is never irrelevant to that wholeness of body, mind and spirit which is God's purpose for us.

When the sermon is over, we follow it with the offer of *a laying on of hands in the name of Christ*—the second characteristic ingredient of a Christian healing service. Even though those of us who minister make absolutely no claim to possessing special individual gifts of healing (see chapters two and six), our experience is that more than 90 percent of those present usually come forward to receive this ministry. In doing so, they are indicating their desire that Jesus should meet them at their point of need, whatever it may be. They may be conscious of a specific physical, mental or spiritual area that needs his touch. There could be a need for the healing of an attitude or relationship or some element in a lifestyle which has slipped away from God. Or they may want to pray for someone near and dear to them. Each individual will have a different reason for needing the touch of Christ.

We never ask why those who come forward have done so. If we were to ask, it might well be a deterrent for some whose need is too embarrassing to admit publicly or too complicated to put into a few words. Also, our aim is not to contemplate our ailments, but to contemplate Christ. So we practice the presence of God and lay on hands in the name of Christ—and we leave him to do his own work in his own way.

Usually we have two pairs of people ministering in this way, one pair for each half of the Communion rail. We minister to each other first, because we need to receive the Lord's healing touch before we can pass it on to anyone else. Each couple usually consists of a member of our staff and a member of the congregation. As those who require ministry come forward and kneel at the rail, we put our hands on their heads gently and firmly and say the words of a short healing prayer together. The touch of four hands and the sound of two voices in unison make it clear that this is not an individual act. It represents the whole body of Christ, giving the touch of Christ. The prayer we most often use in this ministry is "May the healing power of the Holy Spirit be in you. Amen." But it may be varied from time to time: "May the healing power of the Christ child be in you" (at Christmas), "May the healing power of the risen Christ be in you" (at Easter), "Receive a harvest of healing at the hand of God" (at Thanksgiving) or "The Lord Jesus meet you at your point of need" (at any time).

After the laying on of hands, I like to lead my congregation in *a time of devotional prayer*. This is the third key ingredient of a healing service. As I do so, I hold up our church's intercession book—a notebook in which prayer requests have been written down. It is not my practice to include a reading of names or a recitation of ailments. That could lead to negative thinking rather than positive prayer, and, in any event, God knows all those whose names are in the book, and also those whose names should be in but have been left out through ignorance or forgetfulness on our part. So I lift the book, and we practice God's presence and leave the rest to him.

Then we sing a good hymn of praise to end the service, and we make sure that there is no shortage of coffee and people to talk to afterward, just in case there are those present who need to open their hearts.

Getting Started
Some clergy are nervous about holding Christian healing services and

do not know how to start them. I understand these fears and shared them during the earlier days of my ministry. However, in actual fact it is not difficult to start regular healing services. Anyone who has charge of a church has only to follow this simple sequence.

1. Find one other person who is respected in your congregation and who believes in the validity and importance of the healing ministry.

2. Then select a service at which your sermon topic will be the ministry of Christian healing.

3. After the sermon, announce to the congregation that your colleague and you will be administering a laying on of hands to each other during the hymn that will follow and that after you have laid hands on each other you will be available to lay hands on any who may wish to come forward.

4. Explain that you are not trying to pressure anybody into coming forward. God does not require his church to *urge* the laying on of hands in the name of Christ upon anyone, but he does require us to make this ministry *available*.

5. The next month, do the same things again.

While there is no need for the ministrants to worry about whether anyone comes forward or not, in point of fact there has never been an occasion in the many hundreds of Christian healing services which I have led when the invitation has failed to elicit a considerable response—and this includes the scores of services I have taken in churches which had never held a specific "Christian healing service" before.

Inviting People to Respond

The form of invitation to be used might be something like this.

You are welcome to receive a laying on of hands in the name of Christ if you wish to do so for any reason at all.

Perhaps you have been ill in some way and have a need for physical healing. Perhaps you are feeling anxious or depressed and need the touch of Jesus upon your mind. Perhaps some temptation is hard to cope with and you are conscious of the need for healing in the depths of your spirit. Maybe you are conscious of a relationship or an attitude or some element in your lifestyle which needs the healing touch of Christ.

If you wish, you may come forward as an act of commitment, an act of prayer for spiritual deepening, a symbol of your availability to our Lord.

Maybe you want to invite Jesus into your life as Savior, Lord and Friend for the very first time.

Or maybe at this time your mind is on someone else, someone near and dear to you, who has a deep need for the touch of Jesus, and in coming forward you are bringing that person forward in your heart and mind to receive the ministry of healing. You may even want to come forward as a prayer for the healing of society, the healing of the nations.

Or perhaps there is no specific reason why you wish to come forward. You just know that the touch of Jesus is desirable for its own sake, for his own sake, quite apart from any byproducts it may bring. Whatever your reason, you are welcome to the touch of Christ from the body of Christ and to a prayer for the healing power of the Holy Spirit.

If an invitation of this sort is given, and people come forward, and the laying on of hands with prayer is given and received—then what? What is likely to happen? I can only share my own experience.

When we started Christian healing services in my previous parish of St. George's Hyde, there was an instant response. People flocked forward to receive a laying on of hands. There was an instant improvement in the quality of worship. However, there were no instant reports of healing. No healings were reported for a full eighteen months. With hindsight I think this may have been because we were very anxious that there should be healing and were transmitting more of our own anxiety than of the Lord's peace and power.

Nonetheless, the healings did start in time, with help from George Bennett, who came to my parish to conduct a mission of healing and teaching at my request. They started before he came, as the prospect of his presence enabled us to put some of our anxiety aside. The story is told in *Christian Healing Rediscovered* (pp. 14-26).

Since then there has been a steady stream of healing associated both with the services in my own parishes and with services I have been invited to conduct elsewhere.

These healings can be quite spectacular. For instance, a service in a cathedral comes to mind. In the middle of the worship there was great excitement as a woman who could not speak—she had been compelled to give up her job as a teacher because an operation had damaged her vocal cords—suddenly found that her power of speech was totally restored to her. We all knew it had happened when she and the people around her started to praise God with considerable vigor! I met her several times during the years that followed and checked that the healing was permanent and complete.

Often, by contrast, the healings are quiet and go unnoticed at the time. I may find out about them many years later. Yesterday Eira and I were invited to a dinner party, and one of the guests made a point of telling me about her father whom she brought to one of our healing services nineteen years ago, suffering from a depression which was seriously impairing his quality of life. As he went out of church the father told his daughter how much better he felt. In fact, subsequent events showed that his depression began to lift at that point, and he was able to stop all medication. But I would not have known about it had it not been for the chance meeting, nineteen years later, at yesterday's dinner party.

It is a temptation to add a string of similar stories about people who have reported healings of body, mind or spirit following participation in Christian healing services. If I am not careful, at my stage in the healing ministry I can all too easily degenerate into what has been described as a state of anecdotage!

On this occasion I will resist the temptation, because it is better to keep our minds on the Lord—on what he did, what he commanded and what the Scriptures tell us he can enable through the church today.

Results of the Christian healing ministry are his responsibility, and we can absolve ourselves from anxiety on the one hand or pride on the other.

Our responsibility is simply that of obedience.

—TEN—

LISTENING
& COUNSELING

*S*ometimes the way to bring healing to people in distress is not so much by offering them a laying on of hands as by offering a "laying on of ears"!

In chapter four I told the story of Betty, the girl whose vulvitis was a symptom of a deep anxiety based on childhood experiences. Her need was for intensive long-term counseling. It was fortunate that I had been receiving some instruction in basic Christian psychotherapy. It was also fortunate that I knew some of the medical personnel involved in Betty's treatment, so that during the months ahead, while undertaking eight counseling sessions, each lasting about an hour and a half, I was also able to prepare a systematic case history and submit it to Betty's family doctor, to her consultant and to a psychiatrist whom I knew for comments and advice. The result was a lovely, abiding example of Christian healing.

I have in my files many similar case histories, some of them with medical comments appended to them. However, for most of this chapter I propose to make no reference to these files, because "the laying on of ears" which so often provides a channel for Christian healing usually does not depend on professional skills. Not everybody is equipped to counsel. Counseling is a technical procedure, requiring specialist training. However, *everybody* can listen, and the main concern of this chapter is with the healing power of simple listening.

The Power of Listening

I learned about this power as a teenager. I had been invited to attend a residential conference, but on arrival I found I knew hardly anybody there. Everybody else seemed to know one another. They stood around laughing and talking happily. By contrast I felt lonely and insecure, and soon I wanted nothing more than to go home again.

Then it happened—the moment of healing. At supper time an unknown clergyman came into the dining room, collected his own meal and sat down at the table where I was eating mine. He looked at me and said, "I haven't seen you before. Tell me about yourself." I found myself telling him the story of my life. He just listened—but he did so as if I were a person of significance and as though the things which I had to say were important and absorbing. By the time the meal was over, my loneliness and insecurity had gone. I was free to talk to others and listen to others. I have never met him since then, but I have never forgotten him and the healing he brought me.

If you have the time and inclination to listen to others, you have a very precious commodity in your possession. Many doctors would love to have it and feel continually frustrated by their lack of time for patients whose need is not so much for a bottle of pills as for a good long heart-to-heart talk.

Nobody Listened to Vikki

This was the case, for example, with Vikki, a young wife from one of my previous parishes. She was always at her doctor's office. She alternated between losing weight dramatically and putting it on excessively. She suffered from depression and would often burst into tears for no apparent reason. A dose of flu seemed to last forever. She was prone to gastroenteritis. She was accident-prone and broke a bone when she fell. She had breathing difficulties. She had pains in her groin.

As you might imagine, the doctor's pen moved over his prescription pad so rapidly that it almost caught fire! Yet nothing seemed to help.

Before she married she had been perfectly healthy. She enjoyed her school days, and then she enjoyed working as a laboratory assistant; she enjoyed her courtship and engagement; she enjoyed her wedding day.

But then things started to change. She was soon pregnant, and when her son was born she stopped working. She was quickly pregnant again and gave birth to a daughter.

Wayne, her husband, used to go out nearly every night with his friends. He said this was his right because he worked hard to support his family and he needed to relax. Vikki tried to tell him how lonely she felt and how depressed she was beginning to be, but Wayne hardly listened. Then Wayne's work sent him abroad. Vikki was on her own.

Wayne's parents visited her and told her how fortunate she was to have such a fine husband and home! They said it gently and sweetly. She could not bring herself to answer them back. She just became ill.

The problem was that nobody listened to her. Her doctor was too busy. Wayne's parents were too protective toward their son. And Wayne was by now in Ghana!

I left the parish before finding out what happened to Vikki and Wayne, but the prospects for their marriage hardly looked encouraging. In this they are not unique. Nearly half of today's marriages are ending in separation or divorce.

Yesterday evening our parish pastoral committee met, and we spent some time thinking about people like Vikki and Wayne. We are hoping to start a parenting group in connection with a local school. We are hoping that young married people (and not-so-young married people) can come together for useful hints, for a helping hand, and above all because there will always be someone ready to listen. I hope this group will come into being, and that it will prove a channel of healing.

We already provide a similar listening service for the bereaved. In chapter nine I wrote about the healing power of a sensitive Christian funeral service, but I am well aware that this sort of service, important though it is, provides only part of the resources for healing needed by those who have lost someone near and dear to them. They also need to talk about their experiences.

Because of this great need, it is our practice that two weeks after any member of our staff has conducted a funeral service, the chief mourner will receive a letter from me which says,

This letter is to assure you that we are remembering you in prayer each day in this difficult time after your bereavement. We would also count it a privilege to offer you friendship and support.

If you will allow it, one of our congregation will call on you in a few weeks' time to see how things are going and whether there is any practical help we can offer.

Then, unless we have a phone call to say that a visit would not be welcome, one of our members will turn up on the doorstep of the bereaved household—basically to offer the "laying on of ears." Again and again there is an outpouring of pain, of loneliness, perhaps of guilt, perhaps of anger and perhaps of much more beside. There may be some practical action we can take. But first our visitor will listen and, if need be, will go back time after time and keep on listening.

We are often told how much these visits have helped and how much the act of gentle listening can mean.

A Christian Listeners' Network

The Acorn Christian Healing Trust, which exists to promote the healing ministry in England, employs several staff members whose work is to encourage ordinary Christians to become "Christian listeners." Nationwide there are now hundreds of church members who have received basic instruction in the art of being a listener for Christ and who are able to do the sort of work that our parish bereavement visitors do.

According to Shakespeare, after the death of Julius Caesar, Mark Antony said, "Friends, Romans, countrymen—lend me your ears." I believe that Jesus is saying something similar to ordinary Christians today. The Bible tells us to "offer hospitality to one another" (1 Pet 4:9), and in the memorable phrase of Henri Nouwen, listening is "the highest form of hospitality."

Often we Christians are not good at it, and I have to admit that sometimes the clergy can be particularly bad! Dietrich Bonhoeffer wrote, "Christians, especially ministers, so often think they must always contribute something when they are in the company of others, that this is the one service they have to render. They forget that listening can be a greater service than speaking."

So, here and now, pause a while. Open one ear to Jesus and ask him whether at this moment you should open the other ear, unconditionally, unhurriedly, to some person who has deep unspoken needs and for whom your power to listen could provide Christ's channel of healing.

—ELEVEN—

OTHER
MEANS OF
HEALING

*I*f it were allowed to run wild, this chapter could end up as a book in its own right. There is no end to the list of possible means, or channels, of Christian healing. Anything which helps us personally to practice the presence of Jesus is a channel of Christian healing for us. Anything which helps us to communicate the reality of Jesus to other people is a channel of Christian healing for them. (Again, let us be clear that a "channel" for God's work of healing is totally different from the New Age and occult concept of "channeling.")

Some strange things may be included. For example, I am grateful for the inclusion of Acts 19:11-12 in the New Testament. It says, "God did extraordinary miracles through Paul, so that even handkerchiefs and aprons that had touched him were taken to the sick, and their illnesses were cured and the evil spirits left them." It was not that these hand-kerchiefs and aprons were magic, but they reminded people of Paul, and

Paul reminded them of Jesus, and the healing power of Jesus did the rest.

In my last parish there was a household where the family discovered that, as far as they were concerned, there was a healing place on the living-room carpet. It was a place where a much-loved Nigerian curate who spent a year with us used to kneel to pray when he visited them. There was nothing magic about it, but the carpet reminded them of the curate, and the curate reminded them of Jesus, and so when they were in trouble they knelt on the same spot and always felt better for it. They prayed, of course, to Jesus and not to the carpet!

We must never despise or try to discredit another person's individual and unique channel of Christian healing. However, having said that, there are many rather more orthodox channels through which God's healing power can come to us, and it may be of help to list some of them here.

The Bible

It almost goes without saying that *the Bible* itself is a channel of healing. It is good to make sure that our spiritual program involves listening to regular *Bible preaching* of the sort already described in connection with our local Christian healing service.

It is also good to attend a group which meets for the purpose of *Bible-probing*. A well-tried method for such groups is that first a Bible passage is read, then silence is kept. Then three cards are displayed in succession, on which are simple pictures of a candle, a question mark and an arrow. While the candle is displayed, group members share any light which has come to them through the Bible passage. While the question mark is displayed, group members share any questions or problems which the passage has raised for them. Lastly, the arrow is displayed, and group members share any pointers, any guidance which the passage has given to them.

Bible-Praying

We do not have to be together in order for the Bible to be a channel of healing. It can also be so when we study the Bible in solitude—and especially if we incorporate the practice of *Bible-praying* into our personal devotional life. The Ignatian method of Bible-praying has already been described in chapter six, but for those who find that they are not naturally suited to be "Ignatians," there is another method which I can warmly recommend. It does not call upon powers of imagination. It allows the Word of God to do its own work and show its own power.

This prayer method involves selecting a Bible passage, reading it carefully and then being still before it for some minutes, without either exercising the imagination or undertaking any form of proactive mental activity. The odds are that after a first attempt at doing so absolutely nothing will happen, and the next day if the same procedure is followed with the same Scripture passage, probably once again nothing will happen. However, by the third day tiny gleaming lights may begin to shine into your spirit through the text of your passage, and by the fourth day the text could well be ablaze with light and truth and healing.

I can commend this method of Bible-praying because it is the one which I always use to prepare my sermons. I kneel before the Scriptures in prayer day after day, until they themselves speak to me. Then and only then do I take commentary books down off my study shelves and augment the Word of God with the things which others have written about it. The Christian faith tells us that it is the nature of God to communicate.

The method of Bible-praying that I have described—one which I am told embodies an Augustinian rather than an Ignatian approach—allows the Word of God to speak to us directly through Scripture before we listen either to scholarly interpreters or to our own imagination.

The Ministry of Forgiveness

Another key channel of Christian healing is to be found in the church's *forgiveness ministry.* Different denominations express it in different ways, but from a therapeutic viewpoint it does not matter whether God's forgiveness in Christ is discovered within a formal liturgical setting or in an unstructured, informal way.

To accept that we are sinners and to discover that Jesus died upon the cross for our forgiveness, to know that "if we claim to be without sin, we deceive ourselves and the truth is not in us. If we confess our sins, [God] is faithful and just and will forgive us our sins and purify us from all unrighteousness" (1 Jn 1:8-9) brings deep healing with it. The healing can be physical. Jasmine was able to discard her surgical collar when she found forgiveness through Jesus (see *How to Pray When Life Hurts,* pp. 106-7). However, the deepest and most important effect of Christ's forgiveness ministry goes far beyond this world and its ailments. We will take up this theme in chapter thirteen, "Healing for Eternity."

Before leaving the subject of forgiveness, it is worth noting that as well as finding a channel of Christian healing in the church's forgiveness ministry, we will find a further channel if we can be enabled to exercise *our own forgiveness ministry.* We need to be forgiving people as well as forgiven people. The Lord's Prayer takes this for granted. "Forgive us our sins, for we also forgive everyone who sins against us" (Lk 11:4). Until we learn to forgive, we shall always be to some extent in the power of the person we cannot forgive. When we learn to forgive, we will experience freedom and healing at many levels of our being. I have written in greater length about this in chapter four of *How to Pray When Life Hurts.*

Finding Freedom in Giving

Christian giving provides another channel of Christian healing. When we resist the biblical challenge to give proportionately and regularly in the service of God and humankind, not only do we withhold blessings from the church and the world, but we block blessings which God would pour upon our own lives. The prophet Malachi is not one to mince his words in such matters. He tells the people of Jerusalem that God is speaking words of accusation to them. God is saying, "You rob me." When the people ask "How do we rob you?" then God answers bluntly, "In tithes and offerings. You are under a curse—the whole nation of you—because you are robbing me. Bring the whole tithe into the storehouse, that there may be food in my house. Test me in this . . . and see if I will not throw open the floodgates of heaven and pour out so much blessing that you will not have room enough for it" (Mal 3:8-10).

The great thing about Christian giving is that when we accept it as a principle and then practice it in our own life, we dethrone the money-god who can exercise such a baleful effect on us; we sever the bondage which possessions can impose. Jesus says, "You cannot serve both God and Money" (Lk 16:13). Faithful, systematic Christian giving helps us to have our sense of priorities right and releases multilevel blessings. Paul says that if your pattern of life involves cheerful giving you will find yourself "in all things at all times, having all that you need" (2 Cor 9:8). The principle works both ways. "Whoever sows sparingly will also reap sparingly, and whoever sows generously will also reap generously" (2 Cor 9:6).

Fellowship and Service

Christian service and *Christian fellowship* are also natural channels of Christian healing. As an example of both, for many years the church people of Prenton have provided a Christmas dinner party for any who would otherwise be lonely or in need on Christmas Day. After we have worshiped God together on Christmas Eve or Christmas morning, a fleet of cars goes out to collect our guests, a welcoming team receives them in our church hall, a kitchen team provides a full Christmas dinner of turkey and all the trimmings, an entertainment team puts on a Christmas Day variety show, Christmas presents are given, carols are sung, and then the fleet of cars takes our guests home again.

Usually our guests number seventy to eighty people. They often tell us they have found it a happy and healing experience. One year I received a letter from Ethel, an elderly lady who told me that our Christmas party had actually saved her life. Christmas can be the loneliest and most wretched time of the year for those who feel unloved. Ethel wrote that she was actively contemplating suicide when our invitation dropped through her letter-box, but after the experience of love, care and affirmation which she received at St. Stephen's on Christmas Day, she decided that life was worth living after all.

It is not only the recipients who find the Christmas party a happy and healing experience. Those who give up part of their Christmas Day to be on the team that runs the party often say how good Christmas has been and how somehow they have avoided the family squabbles, the boredom, the overindulgence and the sense of pointlessness which can so often spoil Christmas in many households. Jesus said, "It is more blessed to give than to receive" (Acts 20:35), but, of course, in the context of Christian service and Christian fellowship there is blessing in both!

This is only a partial list of channels of Christian healing, and space restrictions require that I now bring it to an end, but not before adding one more—a strange and paradoxical channel.

The Place of Suffering

I am certain that suffering and sickness have no part in God's primary purpose for humankind. When God created the world, we are told he "saw all that he had made, and it was very good" (Gen 1:31). If things had not gone badly wrong, human life would not be characterized by suffering in the way it has come to be.

However, having made this affirmation, I have to recognize that *suffering itself can have a role within God's healing purpose.* It is right to seek healing, but if, for some reason, known or unknown, healing does not come, and if a Christian is moved to offer the experience of suffering to God for him to use, then that suffering itself becomes a power channel through which Christian healing can come to others.

Examples are not difficult to find. Richard Wurmbrand was able to bring a new freedom to many while he himself was in prison, deprived of freedom. Joni Eareckson Tada cannot move because of her quadriplegia, but she has certainly moved many to turn to Christ. David Watson, a leading pastor and speaker in Great Britain, forfeited his life because of terminal cancer, but as he died he was a channel of life to many—and through his books and tapes he still remains so.

It would seem that within God's economy nothing is wasted, not even suffering, sickness and death itself. However, the questions still remain: How can a good God create a world in which so many bad things happen and suffering is such a fact of life? And if healing is God's will, why are some healed and others not?

The healing ministry, like life itself, is full of problems. We turn to face some of them in the next chapter.

TWELVE

PROBLEMS, DIFFICULTIES & FAILURES

W hen I am invited to conduct conferences and missions in connection with the healing ministry, I find that some queries are raised again and again. Here are three of them along with faltering and fallible attempts at answers.

The Question of Suffering

How do you explain the existence of suffering if this world is the creation of a good God?

Usually I would not even try to do so, certainly not while attempting to offer pastoral help to a sufferer. When people are in pain, usually the last thing they need is a philosophical or theological discussion. On these occasions, there is practical wisdom in the old rhyme

Life is mostly froth and bubble

Two things stand like stone

Kindness in another's trouble
Courage in your own.

At a spiritual level, when suffering has to be encountered, many of the deepest and wisest Christians feel it impossible to go any further than to acknowledge that this is a world of mystery. In the words of Henri Nouwen, "Life is not a problem to be solved, but a mystery of wholeness and a mystery of sickness."

I frequently call to mind some words of a dear and wise friend, spoken at a time when I was finding it particularly difficult to deal with certain instances of suffering in my parish and in my own family. "There are times," she said, "when our trust just has to be greater than our understanding."

Having said this, we are still not absolved from bending our limited minds to the difficulties raised by the apparent incompatibility: the existence of pain and evil in a world created by our good God.

This problem has taxed (and eluded) the keenest Christian minds over two millennia. It is unlikely that any comments of mine will add anything of significance to the debate. Still, I feel I must make an attempt. Forgive my inadequacy.

My own conviction is that the mystery of suffering must in some way be related to the mystery of free will.

In our lives we experience both the effects of our own free will and the effects of the free will of others. Free will was, presumably, given to humankind because we were meant to love and be loved—and we can do neither without a measure of freedom. However, because we are a flawed species, again and again our use of free will has been anything but loving. And the result has been pain and grief.

Suffering can perhaps be divided into three categories.

First (and this is the easiest to understand and accept), there is the *suffering we bring on ourselves.* If I drink alcohol excessively, I must not be surprised if the next morning I have a hangover. Proverbs 23:29-

35 contains a graphic description of a hangover: "Who has woe? Who has sorrow? Who has strife? Who has complaints? Who has needless bruises? Who has bloodshot eyes? Those who linger over wine." The writer makes it very clear that if we suffer in this way it will be entirely our own fault, but adds sadly that this does not stop the hung-over man from saying to himself, "When will I wake up so I can find another drink?" The AIDS epidemic provides another—and more deadly—example of people's tendency to suffer from self-inflicted wounds.

Second, there is *suffering we bring on each other.* The AIDS epidemic furnishes an example of this kind as well. Many stress diseases, many road accidents and many diseases connected with pollution provide further examples. Also, in a world that is basically bountiful, so do diseases caused by malnutrition. So do the horrors of war. So do industrial accidents, if health and safety measures are inadequate. So do the traumas suffered by children of broken homes. Wittingly or unwillingly, we use our free will to harm each other as well as ourselves.

This sort of suffering can be seen extending from one generation to another. I think of a lovely young woman I met, born with congenital syphilis and struggling with its ravages. It was no fault of hers. Scripture records an observable fact of life when it points out that children suffer from the sins of their fathers (Ex 20:5).

The third sort of suffering is simply *suffering which does not seem to fit into the first two groups.* It does not seem to have anything to do with the misuse of free will. However, this is a rapidly shrinking list because our increasing knowledge is continually moving ailments and diseases from category three into categories one and two. For instance, lung cancer used to be regarded as a category three complaint, but we now know that our personal smoking habits can make it a category one disease and the passive smoke inflicted on us by others can bring it into category two. It may even be that category three will eventually be abolished.

If we accept the hypothesis that human free will is a major villain in the scenario of suffering, why does God not take our free will away? The answer is not difficult to see. Without free will we would be no more than puppets. If God were to remove our free will, he would destroy us as certainly as if he were to strike each one of us with bolts of lightning.

Moreover, if chapter eight in this book is to be taken seriously, humankind is not the only part of creation to misuse free will. The devil and his demons have also to be taken into account as a source of pain and grief.

If that is a sinister thought, here is a more innocent one.

Clearly, if we are to have a world of beauty and interest, there is bound to be a risk factor involved in human life. If there are mountains and cliffs, there is always a chance someone will fall off them. If there is fire, someone may get burned. If there is water, someone may drown.

It is virtually impossible to envisage a fail-safe world in which nobody could ever possibly suffer hurt.

What Christians can be sure of is that whatever may be the source of suffering, Scripture reveals God as "the Lord who heals" (Ex 15:26).

Healings That Fail

If healing is God's will, why are there sometimes failures in the Christian healing ministry? Why does it not always work instantly and totally?

I have to accept the validity of this question. We have already acknowledged that Christian healing is not a "magic-wand ministry." Personally, I have grave doubts about those who seem to give the impression that there is no failure factor in their healing ministry.

This may be a good point to look back at the story of Fergus at the end of chapter seven. I still remember how angry I felt when he died. I remember waking up and shouting at God in the middle of the night, as I wrestled with my grief and confusion.

I have to admit that I often find myself thoroughly confused. On one occasion a seriously ill person can be totally restored after receiving the ministry of Christian healing. On another occasion there may be no discernible healing whatsoever.

It is not as though I can see any meaningful pattern in the placement of the healings that do take place. Some years ago I was ministering simultaneously to two people who were suffering from what were described as terminal cancers. One was an elderly lady, a Christian widow who was more than ready to join her husband in eternity. Her doctor asked me to go to the hospital and help her die. The other was a young married man with a family dependent on him. My colleagues and I visited both of them. We prayed and laid hands on them both. And there was a spectacular healing: one of the cancers disappeared instantly. It seemed like a miracle.

The strange thing was that the recipient of the miracle was the elderly lady, who is alive to this day and is still pining for her husband, whereas the young man died, and his wife and young children were left to cope with life's considerable difficulties without him. If God had a miracle to spare, it certainly seemed a strange way to allocate it!

There is another sort of failure which I find just as difficult to bear. I think of Bobby and Babs, a married couple who asked me to visit their home because Babs was suffering from a cancer which they had been told was terminal and in its final stages. The hospital had sent her home to die. It was believed that she could have no more than a fortnight of life ahead of her. They were not churchgoers, but they had heard of our healing ministry and sent for me. When I laid hands on Babs and explained that if she held on to Jesus she had nothing to fear in life or death, she smiled and said, "I shall be all right now."

The experience seemed to mean something to her, and I was surprised that I was not asked for any further ministry.

Six years later I happened to meet Bob again when walking in our local park. I said, "How are you?"

He replied, "We are both well."

"Both?" I asked.

"Yes," he said. "The cancer vanished after you laid on hands. X-rays proved it."

I was thrilled and asked if I could visit them. But he said firmly, "No, don't bother. We're not religious people, and we're very busy, but we decided that if we happened to see you it was only fair to mention what had happened!"

Many people might regard that as a success story, but I doubt whether Jesus would have thought so.

The fact is that though I believe that Christian healing is resourced by the might of the Holy Trinity, an honest appraisal of the evidence shows that at physical, mental and spiritual levels there are failures as well as successes.

Why is this so? We must reject overly simplistic answers.

I am sure that it is quite wrong to suppose that a failure of healing must stem from a failure of faith on the part of the recipient. It is also oversimplistic to suppose it must stem from a failure of faith on the part of the ministrant.

It is my equal conviction that those who believe that God's will is sometimes for healing but sometimes not are also being oversimplistic. Our healing God is totally self-consistent. In the words of James, he "does not change like shifting shadows" (Jas 1:17). I may not be able to see God's self-consistency in the way things work out—but then, there is a lot I can't see!

Above all, we must reject the crude notion that suffering is a punishment for sin. Jesus rejected this view decisively (Lk 13:1-4).

So what, if anything, can we say?

If I had to attempt an answer to the enigma, it would be something like this. There are laws governing the universe—laws of logic, laws of nature, laws of life. We are beginning to have a better understanding of some of them, but there is much to learn. God does not break these laws. They are part of his own nature. When we pray for physical healing and it does not happen, some factor within these laws is preventing it. There would be no need to heal in a perfect world, but this sinful world is far from perfect and contains many a block to healing.

I think we can identify some of the maverick factors which serve as blocks to the healing ministry. We cannot rule out that some may be related to the sufferer. There could, for instance, be an unrepented sin. You could not say, "I want to be healed of my hangovers, but I'm going to keep on getting drunk!" But the maverick factor might have nothing to do with the sufferer. It might, for instance, be connected with an atmosphere of negativity with which the sufferer is surrounded at a domestic level. Jesus himself found that his power to work miracles was restricted in Nazareth because of the negative attitude there (Mt 13:53-58). The church itself can also be an unhelpful factor if it fails to be fully aware and obedient. So can our sinful society with its many unhealthy pressures. And who knows what sort of malign influence may come from the mysterious world of principalities and powers?

In the book of Job, after various overly simplistic solutions to the problem of suffering are rejected, Job finally concludes (like my wise friend whom I quoted earlier) that in the last resort his trust has to be greater than his power of understanding (42:3). Paul came to much the same conclusion when his own "thorn in the flesh" was not healed. He knew it came from the devil and not from God. He rightly asked for healing, but when it did not come at a physical level, he just rested in the grace of God (2 Cor 12:7-10). And it certainly did not lessen his own commitment to the healing ministry, as he showed, for instance, during his visit to Malta (Acts 28:7-9).

We too must never turn the difficulties into a reason for opting out of the healing ministry. Think of the medical profession. Every doctor's office would close if one hundred percent success were required as a condition of staying open!

We have to face the problems and failures honestly, without being obsessed with them or allowing them to make us disobedient to the clear command of Christ.

When Is a Healing Miraculous?

If we cannot guarantee total "success" from the Christian healing ministry in every case, how can we know there is supernatural power behind it? Could the results not be due to psychosomatic factors? Or could they not just be coincidences? What evidence is there that miracles can still happen?

Personally, I do not allow myself an excessive use of the word *miracle.* I accept that in many cases a doctor would be able to give a rational explanation of an instance of Christian healing. Look back, for example, at the story of Mildred in chapter four.

Even when I have no medical comment on which to rely, I do not rule out the possibility of a psychosomatic ingredient. A few days ago I visited a parishioner who had suffered stomach pains for a full week. He was taking painkillers without effect. We spent time talking together about the considerable problems in his life, and then it seemed right to pray with him and lay on hands. As I did so, the pain left him—a fact he celebrated by giving me a bag of splendid home-grown tomatoes. I am well aware that there could possibly have been psychosomatic factors involved.

However, it would be difficult to explain the two cases of disappearing cancers earlier in this chapter in psychosomatic terms. You could, I suppose, speak about "spontaneous remissions" and regard the timing as coincidental, but I cannot help recalling the famous words of Archbishop William Temple, "I find that when I pray, coincidences happen, and when I stop praying, coincidences stop happening!"

It is even more difficult to think of the case of Roger in chapter seven in terms of coincidence, or the local dentist in chapter three, or the woman "as good as dead" in chapter six. It did seem in each case that there was an element of the miraculous at work—not that God was breaking his own laws but that he was drawing upon laws so deep and mysterious as to be totally beyond my understanding.

Before ending this chapter, let me add one more story. If you can think of a rational explanation for it, do let me know. For myself, in spite of all my normal reluctance to speak in terms of miracles, I can find no other word for it.

Percy turned up on my doorstep one day in a state of great agitation. His daughter Rowena had attempted suicide and was in the intensive care unit of a local hospital after taking a drug overdose.

Her life was hanging in the balance. Percy told me she could die any time. He pleaded with me to go to the hospital.

For some reason, which I cannot now even remember, I could not leave the house instantly, but I promised to go just as soon as I could. Percy drove back to the hospital, and a quarter of an hour later I followed him in my car. It was about a ten-minute journey.

On arriving at the intensive care unit, I was shown to the bed on which Rowena's pale, inert body was lying. She was surrounded by worried-looking medics who told me that her condition was critical and that they had no idea whether she would live or die. I took her hand in mine and started to talk to her, telling her that her life was not meant to end like this, that there were things ahead which she was meant to see and do and be. "Rowena," I said, "in the name of Jesus, come back to us. In the name of Jesus—*open your eyes.*" And she did.

For fifteen minutes or so, I stayed by her bed and held her hand and talked to her and prayed for her, until one of the doctors said that it was safe for me to leave her. "She's past the crisis," he said. "She'll be all right now."

As I left the ward I met Percy and told him that he need not worry, that I had spent a quarter of an hour with Rowena, talking to her and praying for her, and that I had been assured she would now be all right. He gave me the strangest look, and so I repeated my words of assurance before I left. A few days later, he came to see me.

"You may wonder," he said, "at the strange look I gave you at the hospital. The reason is that when I left your vicarage I drove at breakneck speed to the hospital and rushed to intensive care to wait for you— only to find that all was well and that you had been there with Rowena for a quarter of an hour!"

Percy and I looked at each other blankly. Rowena's reawakening had been startling enough in itself, but the apparent time-warp factor in the situation, which had allowed me to arrive just when I was needed, was completely beyond us.

It still is.

—THIRTEEN—

HEALING
FOR ETERNITY

*T*hey had had quite a time of it, the seventy-two disciples. Jesus had sent them out to heal the sick and to preach the kingdom of God in his name. They must have been frightened, but they were obedient. And it had all worked out well—amazingly well. Even demons submitted to them when they ministered in the power of the name of Jesus.

So it was that they came back rejoicing, thrilled to the core. Jesus was thrilled too. He said, "I saw Satan fall like lightning from heaven. I have given you authority to trample on snakes and scorpions and to overcome all the power of the enemy; nothing will harm you" (Lk 10:18-19).

But then he put it all into perspective. "However, do not rejoice that the spirits submit to you, but rejoice that your names are written in heaven" (v. 20).

Every other form of Christian healing pales into insignificance beside the healing of the human soul.

"God so loved the world that he gave his one and only Son, that whoever believes in him shall not perish but have eternal life" (Jn 3:16). That is healing indeed. That is healing in depth. That is healing for eternity.

Mrs. Frances Alexander's fine old hymn puts it simply and beautifully.

> There is a green hill far away,
>   Without a city wall,
> Where the dear Lord was crucified
>   Who died to save us all.

> We may not know, we cannot tell,
>   What pains he had to bear,
> But we believe it was for us
>   He hung and suffered there.

> He died that we might be forgiven,
>   He died to make us good,
> That we might go at last to heaven,
>   Saved by his precious Blood.

> There was no other good enough
>   To pay the price of sin,
> He only could unlock the gate
>   Of heaven and let us in.

> O dearly, dearly has he loved,
>   And we must love him too,
> And trust in his redeeming blood,
>   And try his work to do.

Unless the contents of this book are put within the context of the words of that hymn, everything I have written will be partial and unbalanced.

A Most Amazing Offer

Because we human beings have fallen away from God, we are souls at risk. Our whole species is in peril. But the amazing claim of the Christian gospel is that God cares enough about us, in spite of our follies and sins and self-destructiveness, that in Jesus Christ, at immense and unfathomable cost, he has made the most amazing offer that could be conceived in or beyond this world.

We are invited to place our hand in the pierced hand of Jesus so that he can lead us through this life, whatever it may bring, and then into death, through death, and into the mystery of eternity.

The Christian claim and conviction is that wherever we travel with Jesus in time or eternity, we can travel without fear. We can travel with optimism, with expectancy that the best is yet to be and that we do not know a fraction of it yet. It is all too much to put into words. "No eye has seen, no ear has heard, no mind has conceived what God has prepared for those who love him" (1 Cor 2:9).

But as always, he will force none of this on us. As always, he waits upon our free will.

There is a prayer which we often use at our Christian healing services. It can be used to take a first step toward Jesus, but it can also be used again and again by those who wish to reaffirm Christian commitment and ask for closer union with the Lord.

I am going to pray it now for myself—and I invite you to pray it with me.

Jesus, I know that I am a sinner, and I am truly sorry for the wrongs I have done, but I also know that you love me and gave yourself for me. You offer to come into my life if I will let you in. You offer healing for the sins and hurts of my soul. You offer to feed me with your own truth.

Gratefully I accept your offer to be my Savior, Lord and Friend. I ask for forgiveness. I put my trust in you and want you to work in me, healing me, feeding me, living in me.

Help me to use my life in your service. Thank you for all you are going to do in me. Amen.

YOU ARE THE BODY OF CHRIST

S t. Stephen's and St. Alban's Prenton are not megachurches. They do not have massive congregations. Anything they can do, your church can also do. Anything I can do as an individual, you can do too—and perhaps you can do it better.

You and I may have little to contribute to the healing ministry in our own strength. The good news is that we need little.

Jesus is the provider in the ministry of Christian healing—as he is in every aspect of gospel life and experience.

Jesus was never a nonevent. That is why the church should never be a nonevent.

If we have accepted his invitation to belong to his church, we are his body. We are called to speak his Word, communicate his touch, receive and share his love, stand for his principles, share his pain and be infectious with his life and his healing.

If we disregard this commission, we will have become irrelevant to or even enemies of Jesus. But if we accept it, we cannot begin to imagine the adventure, the healing activity and the fearful glory that may lie ahead.

To every Christian the commission of Scripture is clear. "You are the body of Christ." All that remains is for us to become what we are!